become a
psychic
wanderer

About the Authors

Kathryn Harwig (Minneapolis, MN) is a professional psychic medium and appears at expos, conferences, and events worldwide. She has written a monthly column for *The Edge* magazine, is a regular guest on radio, and has appeared on A&E's *The Unexplained* and Court TV's *Psychic Detectives*. She has traveled to more than ninety countries. Visit her online at Harwig.com.

Jean Harwig (Minneapolis, MN) grew up telling fortunes with tarot cards and talking to dead relatives. She holds a Bachelor's degree in Social Work and Religious Studies and has worked as a social worker with the developmentally disabled for over twenty years. She has studied with Starhawk and Z Budapest and has had an audience with His Holiness the Dalai Lama. Though her home will always be Minneapolis, Minnesota, Jean dedicates a large portion of her time to travel and has visited more than fifty countries.

Expand Your Mind & Soul Through Travel

become a psychic wanderer

KATHRYN HARWIG & JEAN HARWIG

Llewellyn Publications
Woodbury, Minnesota

FIRST EDITION
First Printing, 2013

Book design by Donna Burch
Cover design by Kevin R. Brown
Cover images: iStockphoto.com/20196194/Simone Becchetti
            iStockphoto.com/17711902/Yulia Polischuk
Editing by Connie Hill
Interior compass from Art Explosion
Interior photos provided by the authors

Llewellyn Publications is a registered trademark of Llewellyn Worldwide Ltd.

Library of Congress Cataloging-in-Publication Data

Harwig, Kathryn, 1951–
  Become a psychic wanderer : expand your mind & soul through travel / Kathryn Harwig & Jean Harwig. — First Edition.
    pages   cm
  ISBN 978-0-7387-3338-8
1. Parapsychology. 2. Psychics. I. Title.
  BF1031.H293   2013
  133.9'1—dc23   2013010612

Llewellyn Publications
A Division of Llewellyn Worldwide Ltd.
2143 Wooddale Drive
Woodbury, MN 55125-2989
www.llewellyn.com

Printed in the United States of America

Other books by Kathryn Harwig

Published by Llewellyn Publications
The Return of Intuition (2010)

Published by Spring Press:
Your Life in the Palm of Your Hand (1994)
The Millennium Effect (1996)
The Intuitive Advantage (2000)
The Angel in the Big Pink Hat (2005)
Palm Visions (2008)

Published by Insight:
Invest in Joy
with co-author Dorothy Lee (2009)

*To our favorite companions in life
and on our many journeys, Fred and Loren,
and to all the wonderful psychic wanderers
who have joined us on our travels.*

Contents

Ever since happiness heard your name
It has been running through the
streets trying to find you.

—HAFIZ

Introduction

Pines were about the only things that grew well in the rocky soil of Pine County, Minnesota, where my co-author, sister, and best friend Jean and I grew up. Our father was a rather halfhearted farmer. He far preferred scouring estate sales and auctions to plowing fields. We were poor, at least by today's standards, although so was everyone else we knew so it didn't seem to bother us a lot.

I was a dreamy, sickly little girl suffering from severe asthma and was allergic to just about everything. In the 1950s asthmatic kids were told not to exercise or play, so I spent a great deal of my early childhood lying on the couch and watching old movies on our tiny black and white television.

The *Road to...* movies with Bing Crosby and Bob Hope were my all-time favorite movies. Lying there, dreaming of all the exotic destinations in the movies, I never really believed that a poor, sickly kid from Pine County would get beyond the big city of Minneapolis. Still, in my imagination I was Dorothy Lamour, wearing a sarong and heading off to Bali and Rio and Zanzibar.

In my heart I longed to be a gypsy. From birth, I had an unexplainable fascination with people's palms. By the age of four or five years, I had discovered that I could learn about a person simply by looking at their palm. The lines, particularly those in the hands of my grandmother's elderly friends, fascinated me. "Look," I would say to them while pointing to a line, "this is when you got married and these are your children." I was surprised that they couldn't see what to me was in plain sight.

Our family had a love-hate relationship with intuition. Astrology and all things mystical fascinated our mother, but we belonged to a fundamentalist Christian church that taught that such things were of the devil. We were told by the church that fortunetelling and psychic ability were evil, yet my experience was that these things were good and helpful. It seemed prudent to keep my ideas and experiences to myself. My health improved in my teens and by the time I finished high school, all I wanted out of Pine County was to get out of Pine County. I went off to college, majored in psychology, and married at age twenty-one. My inherent psychic abilities and palmistry skills were buried as my secret, and my focus was my goal of living a normal life. Then, on my first job, as a new probation officer, I discovered myself secretly using my intuitive abilities to read and figure out my probationers. After a few years, my husband, Loren, and I decided to attend law school.

For four years I worked full-time as a probation officer while attending law school four nights a week. Weekends were devoted to studying. There was no time for things like intuition or spirituality. I learned that staying very busy quieted the nagging voice of intuition. In fact, if my life pace was frantic enough, that whisper even became inaudible for a time. I would soon learn that ignoring the voice would cause it to return with a shout.

Six weeks before our graduation from law school, my life took an irrevocable turn. My husband and I were having a rare meal at home together when I felt a sudden and intense pain in my chest. Unable to trace a cause, I waited until the pain was unbearable before Loren rushed me screaming to the emergency room. I spent the last six weeks of my law school education in the intensive care unit. Although I was allowed to graduate with my class, I never returned to the school. The perforated esophagus, along with the out-of-body experience I had prior to surgery, would change my life in ways I could never imagine.

I read once that if you live when you should have died, you will never look at life in the same way. That was certainly true for me. My recovery from my illness, though lengthy, became complete, but I could not look at life in the same way. I developed an overriding passion to experience the world. I changed from being a woman who had barely left the state of Minnesota to a person who spent much of her disposable cash and time traveling the world. I felt driven to see and to do things that I'd previously had no interest in experiencing.

I felt I could no longer deny who I was. I allowed my natural intuitive gifts to come out of the closet and, over a period of years, I wrote many books about intuitive subjects and trained thousands of people to develop their psychic gifts.

My husband and I started a very successful law practice, but my heart was always drawn to my intuitive work. My law and psychology degrees gave me credibility to speak to groups who might not otherwise have been interested in intuition. Soon, I was being called to train police, teachers, secretaries, correction workers, and business and professional people. Many in these groups were skeptical, but all were curious. At some level, few of us deny the reality of intuition. Our own experiences verify its existence to us. I have met very few people who have not had intuitive moments … times when they just know something without knowing exactly how they know it. My goal has been and continues to be to train people to use their intuition, no matter where they are. Intuition can become a regular, reliable, controllable, and predictable tool that makes life easier.

As part of my training programs I am privileged to be able to lead groups on spiritual journeys all over the world. Traveling and intuition are my passions and being able to combine them is a blessing I am grateful for each day of my life. It is also a joy and privilege to travel with people who have an open mind and are on a quest to understand and train their intuitive skills.

Once travel gets in your blood, it is surprising what a priority it becomes in your life. I measure what things cost in trips rather than dollars. For example, recently I was debating a new sofa but decided against it since it would cost almost an entire trip. Because of that passion, I have a rather shabby living room but a very full passport.

My travel lust rubbed off on my younger sister, Jean, a long time ago. She, along with her husband, Fred, and my husband, Loren, are my most frequent travel companions. We have dreamed of writing a book together for many years. I was, I will admit, a bit concerned because we had no idea how to co-author a book. Would we argue? How was it even done? Like everything we have done together in life we figured it out as we went along. Early in the writing process we decided we would both just tell our stories in our own unique voices and writing styles. Here is Jean's explanation for how this book came into being:

The genesis of this book was in a sidewalk café where Kathryn and I were indulging in our favorite activities: discussing spirituality and finalizing plans for our next trip while drinking endless cups of coffee. Along with our husbands, we were going to Brazil the next week. We were taking different flights and meeting in a little town along the Amazon. As we climbed into our cars I shouted, "Meet me in Manaus!" Kathryn said, "Now that is a book title."

Since that moment Kathryn and I have talked about our passions many, many times. Many of our discussions have found their way into this book, along with more than a few rules for making travel more rewarding spiritually.

It is astonishing to me that I have seen so much of the world. It is yet more astonishing that my spiritual path has become so intertwined with my travel. For me, travel IS a spiritual practice, a meditation, and an observance of living in the here and now. When I remove myself from the day to day, I can focus on the moment. When I challenge myself to find the sacred in a mosque or on a mountain I find out more about myself and my Creator. I feel that each trip is a pilgrimage into the divine (although that is very hard to believe when I am in an airport).

As Kathryn has written, our childhoods were a strange mix of fundamental Christianity and mysticism. It seemed quite normal to me to attend Sunday church as a family and then come home and work the Ouija board. My grandmother and mother would read our horoscopes out loud from the paper right after reading the daily devotional bible reading.

Looking back, I can see that our relatives had a deep love and relationship with Christ. Still, their heritage and strong, innate psychic abilities refused to let them close the door on the unknown. It all worked together in a strange, effective harmony most of the time. Whether it was Edgar Cayce's predictions or a traveling evangelist's date for the rapture, my family recognized that the universe had mystery and magic.

My grandfather was half Sami, the indigenous people of Sweden and Norway. His mother had been a healer when they first came to Minnesota. Ojibwe Indians would camp by her cabin on the banks of the Rum River, and they would trade medicines and charms back and forth. Her son, my Grandpa Eph, deeply believed that God had created little people (what we call elementals) and earth spirits; he could see them and taught us how to ask for their help. His brother, Dewey, always said to me, "I do not need to go to church and pray so everyone can see how holy I am. I just need to walk in the woods to find God. He and I talk privately."

My grandmother, Ruth, was what I would call a kitchen mystic or generational witch. She had a ritual or spell for everything and every situation. Of course, she would then follow it up with a prayer to Jesus. Rosemary had to grow by the front door for protection, a turned-up hem meant a powerful wish for the wearer of the dress, and if a bird hit the window we anxiously waited for news of who had died. When I was sixteen she removed her wedding ring and gave it to me, saying, "This will always bless and protect you. I will always be with you." I have worn it daily since then, feeling her ever-watchful love shielding me.

Then, of course, there were my mother's cousins who would blow in from California and New York to take us hunting for alien space ships while discussing their past lives with us. Cousin Kenneth called us within minutes of my grandmother's passing. "Aunt Ruth just died, didn't she?' he asked. "I saw her walking with my father (who had died two years before) and their mother."

So, I grew up telling fortunes with the Tarot cards I received for Christmas and talking to dead relatives. I realized when I was very young that if I listened I would hear stories and truths from those who had passed on. I filled my bedroom walls with their photographs and often confused my older relatives by knowing facts from a distant past that I could not have known.

With age came the desire to conform to the very rigid confines of our church and community. I learned when and where it was safe to talk about the things I had experienced. I soon found that a sure way to tune out my abilities was to use alcohol, and for ten years I drank nearly daily.

At the age of seventeen a friend and I were driving far too fast down a rainy, windy road, after dark. Suddenly, on a nearly missed curve in the road, the car rolled over and I was thrown through the passenger window almost fifty feet into a ditch (wearing seat belts was not an expectation at this time). I honestly do not remember the accident, just waking up in a ditch in pain. I was immediately transported from our local hospital to the trauma center in Minneapolis, about an hour and a half from Pine City.

The pain was amazing and overwhelming. I must have been in shock because I have never been so cold. What bothered me most, however, was the itching of the sand that was embedded in my scalp.

Soon I lay in ICU, hooked up to many monitors. Suddenly, the pain stopped and I was filled with euphoria. I absolutely knew that everything was all right and I was loved and cherished. My grandmother, who had died the year before after being wheel-chair bound, walked in and took my hand, that wore her wedding ring, in hers.

"Darling girl, it is not time for you to go yet. You have too much to accomplish and see," she said to me. I argued with her, because the last place I wanted to be was back in that hospital bed. Gently, she put my hand down and I returned to consciousness. All the monitors were beeping and there was a very anxious team of medical professionals standing around me. I was back.

Shortly afterward my mother and two sisters came in. At the time that I "died" they had been praying for me with our pastor in the waiting room.

I had broken almost all of the bones on the right hand side of my body. My leg was broken in two places and my arm was shattered and required two surgeries and the placement of a metal plate to heal it. My back was cracked in two places and my ribs had punctured my lungs (that is what ultimately caused me to die for those few minutes). Recovery was long and hard. I missed most of my senior year of high school, but I walked across the stage to get my diploma! I think that experience, which was amazingly frightening and painful, was also part of the impetus that caused me to devote so much of my life to spiritual wandering.

I have traveled on many paths since my childhood, but I know that my early years truly formed the basis for my spiritual beliefs. I have a knowing that is strong and deep that I am connected and protected by this earth and her Creator.

I have been blessed to study many belief systems, starting with a minor in Comparative Religion when I studied Social Work at Augsburg College. I also have been blessed to study with Starhawk and Z Budapest, two of the most influential women in the field of Wiccan Religion, as well as meeting countless wise women who enriched my understanding of Spirit. I have sat in a crowded room listening to the Dalai Lama, lit a candle to the Virgin in an abandoned church in Turkey and received my spirit name from a Lakota Elder in a sweat lodge in the north woods. Each experience brought me a bit closer to knowing myself and my God.

The wisest words I ever heard were "All paths lead to the same God." The more I have studied the more I have found that the core tenets of all major religions are the same. I truly believe in a compassionate and loving God, but also believe there is no one exclusive path to finding him/her. The Divine does not need our worship and rituals, it is we who need the rituals and meditations to bring us closer to the Divine.

I believe with my entire being that we are spiritual entities having a physical experience. So it makes no sense for us to confine our religious practices to a full moon or Sunday service. Every breath is sacred, every act a chance to worship. As I accepted this I learned that I could also strengthen and refine any intuitive abilities on a daily basis simply by being present and paying attention!

Spirit eventually led me to a place where I could face the world without alcohol as a crutch, and I now have thirty years of sobriety. I mention this because it is a huge part of my relationship to the Divine and to others. It was certainly grace that helped me to quit blocking out the world and to embrace any abilities that I have been given.

For me, travel is a spiritual practice. I most often put away the busyness of everyday life and allow myself to connect with the Divine when I am traveling. I see new things with fresh eyes, learn new ways of thinking from new acquaintances, and challenge myself to confront my complacency. Traveling gives me the time to sit for an hour by the lake and study its stillness. Being a psychic wanderer allows me time to wonder at the complexity and simplicity of our Earth.

There is no "autopilot" when I am traveling, I have to stay in the here and now. That is the greatest gift of the journey for me. The trip does not need to be exotic—one of my most sacred experiences came from a day trip to Pipe-stone, Minnesota. One just needs to be open to the moment.

To make it easier for you to know which of us is speaking, Jean's stories are italicized and mine are in the regular font.

chapter one

Not all who wander are lost.
—J. R. R. TOLKIEN

What Is a Psychic Wanderer?

Traveling, whether around the corner or around the world, is one of the best ways to enhance psychic ability. New views and experiences open our minds to look beneath and beyond our typical worldview. It challenges us to see beyond normal vision, to hear between the words and to intuitively know things outside of our five senses. There is no faster route, in my opinion, to becoming an intuitive master. To become a psychic wanderer, you must learn to see the world with new eyes. It is not necessary to travel abroad or even out of your neighborhood. What is important is to be more than a tourist in your own life. Psychic wanderers use their third, intuitive eye to view the world in a different way. They learn to take new and uncharted routes, wander with the goal of seeing rather than being intent on a set path, ask intuitive questions while trusting that the answers will appear, and boldly try new things. Becoming a psychic wanderer will enhance your life in ways you can hardly dream.

While visiting exotic locales provides many opportunities for opening one's third eye, the same thing can be experienced in any location, if viewed with new, open, and inquisitive eyes. The key is to set the intention to become a psychic wanderer, adventurer, and traveler. As Jean's and my stories illustrate, this intention often gets set after a life-changing illness or experience. However, you can set the intention right now, simply with your desire to see more of the world with all of your eyes…no matter where you are.

When you decide to view your life's journey as an adventure, using all of your senses, embracing new experiences with gusto, and honing your intuitive skills, you are doing psychic wandering. All the tools you need to develop this skill will be discussed in this book. Your destination becomes irrelevant. The wandering, learning, knowing, and using your psychic skills are what is important.

As a psychic wanderer, you have an edge and an advantage. You intuitively know if there is trouble ahead or if protection is necessary. You travel through life with the confidence of an experienced adventurer. The road becomes smooth and safe, even when the map shows danger and obstacles.

Becoming a psychic wanderer doesn't take time or money, although both of those come in handy, of course. Mostly, what it takes is a sense of adventure and a willingness to see yourself as such. Manifesting travel begins and ends in your imagination, heart, and soul. Below, Jean describes how she manifests her trips.

My oldest sister, Ruth, died very unexpectedly when I was 37. To say it was a life-changing event for our family is an understatement. For me it was a real wake-up call. Her death taught me a huge lesson in manifesting my travel dreams. I began to picture myself traveling, and to repeat an affirmation inviting travel into my life.

My husband and I had never really traveled in the ten years we had been together. Our focus was on establishing a family and a life together. After my sister's death, though, we realized that tomorrow was not a given. She had never left the state of Minnesota, but always had huge dreams of traveling the globe. She often signed up for travel brochures to come to our house in her name, just a quirk we had come to expect from her. About two months after her funeral we received a mimeographed brochure from a small start-up tour company out of New York City. Getting mail addressed to my deceased sister got my attention. They offered a ten-day tour of China, including all airfare, for $999. This was one of the first open tours offered to communist China, a place I had never intended to visit.

Also in the mail was a check from a one-time friend, now acquaintance, for $1,000 she had borrowed from me six years earlier. I had never thought to see the money back, and here it was delivered out of the blue.

Needless to say, the Universe had thumped me on the head and said, "You are to do this." More amazingly, my husband, sister Kathryn, brother James and sister-in-law Mary all accompanied me to China three months later. It was astonishing that everything seamlessly moved forward exactly as it should have.

When I took my job as a social worker for Hennepin County a few years before I had decorated my cubicle with glossy calendar pages showing world landmarks. Right above my desk I had pinned a 12"x12" photo of the Great Wall of China. I sat and looked at that picture, without really seeing it, for hours a day. I had also pinned up the Taj Mahal and a view of a Balinese rice terrace. I never would have guessed that within three years I would have traveled to all three of those destinations.

I truly believe that the Universe will give us what we ask for, so be very careful to ask for what will bring you happiness and health, for that which will enrich the world and others around you.

Intent is powerful and when we focus our intent we create miracles. Intent can be called by many names: manifesting, prayer, spell, Feng Shui, magic … it all springs from the same core. There is great power in knowing and naming your intention, then expecting the Universe to create it.

Steps to Manifesting

1: Know your overarching goal

If you were to ask me right now what I most need I would say to lose weight. It has been a struggle and a burden for me for years. So why can't I find the diet, manifest the program, magically cast a spell to help me into that size six dress?

Because I do not truly desire it. Somewhere in the back of my reality is the memory of how I was treated and how I acted when I was slender. I had given up a lot of my power as a woman to be and act sexy. Although I understand that losing weight now would not make me the person I was twenty years ago, I do not believe that I truly KNOW that. A part of my soul says, "Hey, you are happy, pretty, and powerful just the way you are now. Don't give any of that up just to be skinny."

My overarching goal is to be healthy and active, and I am. My doctor assures me I am in good health with no concerns, my weekends are spent gardening and walking. My strong body carries me upstairs with ease and lets me play piggyback with my nieces. The truth is that I am not ready to lose the weight. To me being skinny means wearing uncomfortable high heels and Spanx, sucking my stomach in and worrying about what people think of me. Deep down I am enjoying elastic waistbands and ice cream. Until I am ready to embrace a new view of myself, I cannot manifest it.

So spend some time asking yourself, "What do I truly want from life?" If you immediately think you want to be rich, dig deeper and find out what that means to you. It probably doesn't mean a new Ferrari or a bigger house. Does it mean security, freedom, generosity? Then those are the overarching goals you need to manifest.

2: Create an affirmation or mantra that supports your goal

Create a short, positive phrase that states what you want. Since the Creator has given us unlimited power to affect our world, be sure that you are not limiting what the Universe can bring into being. Always state your affirmation as occurring in the present, and search to find the overarching goal behind it.

My personal affirmation for manifesting trips is, "I invite travel and adventure into my life." How simple is that? Yet how powerful.

If you want to go to Paris, of course you could affirm, "I enjoy being in Paris" and I have no doubt that you will bring that into reality. Instead, leave some space for serendipity and the knowledge of the divine to truly bring you what you need. Instead of spending a week in Paris, the Universe may want you to spend the summer working in a small town in Belgium with many weekends in Paris.

Now repeat your mantra as often as you can. For me, the best moments are when I am falling asleep and awakening. I can literally feel the power of my thoughts connecting with the Universe. If you meditate or spend a daily time in prayer or ritual, take time to include your affirmation and reinforce your intent. I also repeat my affirmation when I am driving, or waiting in a doctor's office, or any time I have a moment to connect with my subconscious and begin manifesting.

3: Support your affirmations with joyful reminders

Create a place where you have travel mementos of past trips or pictures of travel you would like to do in the future. Buy a replica of the Eiffel Tower for your desk at work. Instead of feeling jealous or bitter about other people's travel experiences, EMBRACE their stories and feel their joy. Envision yourself as doing the things they are telling you about and going to the same destinations. Set up an account or jar to put saved money in for the express purpose *of travel, then watch the cash flow in and feel the reality coming into being.*

4: Live in gratitude

For me, this is the key to bringing your wishes into being. What we focus on becomes our reality. We all know of the unhappy millionaire. I have been blessed to know people living in straw huts and eating potatoes with goat's blood who are joyful. Truly, it is our attitude that creates the life we will live.

Sarah Ban Breathnach's books introduced the concept of a gratitude journal to me years ago. It has changed my life. Simply spend a few minutes at the end of each day thinking about what went right, what you were blessed with, what you are grateful for. Briefly list three things.

Some days are challenging. I must admit to writing, "I am still breathing" on more than one occasion. Still, this simple exercise slowly rewires your brain to feel gratitude and focus on the positive. If you want positive things to come to you, you must feel gratitude in the here and now.

5: Accept that the Universe and you are bringing your goal into being

We always look outside ourselves for answers and solutions, but truly we hold these within. Trust that the Creator will hear your intention and help you to create the reality you want. Do not limit yourself by looking for specific outward signs of your wishes becoming manifested. Spirit has much bigger and better solutions, ones we cannot consciously fathom.

Allow the process to happen. Practice patience.

6: Make it happen

While you are being patient, also take specific steps toward your goals. "God helps those who help themselves," as our mother always used to say. If you want to travel more you need to make that your priority on a conscious level as well. Pass up that latte and put the $3 in an envelope labeled "dinner at the Moulin Rouge." Decide to eat a peanut butter sandwich for dinner instead of going out to eat. Spend endless hours on the internet looking for a cheap tour company or a rental house in the south of France.

Ultimately, we are each responsible for our dreams and making them come true. Don't limit yourself, act in gratitude and joy, and share your joy with others.

One you have learned to manifest the journey, the next step is to learn how to see the destination with the eyes of a psychic wanderer. That is the purpose of this book.

What Is the Third Eye?

The third eye, sometimes known as the inner eye or the sixth chakra, is said to be the place on the body where we see visions, experience clairvoyance and access inner realms. Many people believe that there is actually an organ called a third eye, situated slightly above and centered between your actual eyes. Some speculate it is a type of gland, roughly the size of a pea, and that it controls our ability to see visions outside of normal eyesight. It is also called clairvoyance.

I have no idea if there is a physiological explanation for the third eye. I do know, from experience, that there are means by which we can open up our senses to allow for better psychic vision and knowledge. We all have access to our third eye constantly, although the act of traveling provides us with many more opportunities than usual to use our third eye and cultivate our inner vision. Everyone has had the experience of going through the day on autopilot, not even noticing our surroundings. Most of us have had instances where we have driven to a familiar and routine destination with no conscious awareness of how we got there or what we saw along the way. Traveling in an unfamiliar and unknown environment keeps us from doing that. In order to function as a psychic wanderer, we must keep all of our senses—including our third eye—open and aware. This openness and awareness brings many more opportunities for practicing, developing, and cultivating our inherent psychic ability.

Boudhanath Stupa in Nepal.

Try Taking Different Routes

One easy way to start this process is to start driving different routes, even if you are heading to a familiar destination. Try taking the side roads to work or driving a few blocks out of your way to the store. Take a walk on streets that you haven't walked down for a long time, if ever. As you do this, notice how much more aware you become. Because you are taking a different route, your brain can't switch into auto pilot. You are much more likely to notice new things such as a new color of paint on a building or a billboard you have never seen before. The reason you notice a particular thing is that your third eye is giving you a message by causing you to focus on it, out of all the hundreds of things it could have chosen. Trust this to be true and assume that the thing on which your eye focused, does, indeed, have something to say to you. Then, ask yourself a simple question: "What message could this be giving me for my day today?"

For example, perhaps you take a new route to work and intuitively notice a building with many broken windows and shabby, peeling paint. You might then ask yourself: "What in my life is beginning to feel worn and shabby?" You might know the meaning of what your third eye was drawn to immediately and understand your message or you might need to ask for yet another message. If so, ask your third eye to find another message, this time giving more information. You will be amazed at how many messages you can get on a ten-minute walk. Psychic wandering can be done in very short doses, as well as month-long pilgrimages.

The act of traveling teaches the wanderer many lessons. In our wanderings throughout the world Jean and I have learned things that would have been difficult to experience in any other fashion. We will share these lessons with you, as well as describe ways you can experience the same result wherever you may go. We will also give you exercises that can be done anywhere and at any time. These exercises will aid you in enhancing your psychic ability, paying attention to your intuitive messages and in learning about yourself, your relationships, and your life's path.

Pilgrimages and Sacred Sites

For as long as humans have existed on this planet, we have been wanderers. Long before our species gathered in settlements, learning to plant and raise food, and herd animals, we were hunters and gatherers. Living in small tribes, we would wander as far as we could walk, searching for food, shelter, and adventure. In this nomadic time of our heritage, we had no security, no home base and little to guide us except our third eye and psychic ability.

Of course, no one today really knows the motivation that prompted this lifestyle and it is likely that hunger and survival were the main motivators. What I believe, though, is that these early humans also had a genetic component that prompted them to wander and see the world. I also believe that this same inherited gene calls us to do the same. Our ancient ancestors needed to keep their third eyes open because the world was a dangerous place and not paying attention could cost them their lives. They also had to use their intuitive senses to determine which plants were edible and which were poisonous. They used their inner guidance to navigate by the stars and plan by the seasons. They were consummate intuitive beings.

As long as humans have stayed close to the earth, they also have stayed close to their psychic roots. Even when we settled down from our nomadic lifestyles and built farms and villages, we still charted our lives by the seasons and wandered when we could. Then, with the advent of the industrial revolution, we started living our lives in small boxes and working in larger ones. Our lives became more predictable and stable. We could relax a little when surrounded by security and could turn down our psychic warning system. Unfortunately, some people turned the volume so low that they forgot they had the ability at all. Those who wanted to awaken their intuitive ability would often embark on a pilgrimage or psychic wandering. Often it was going out for a walk in the woods or a short retreat. Sometimes it was a year-long journey to a foreign land. Human psychology contains an innate urge for adventure. For as long as there has been history, human beings have been psychic wanderers, often labeling these journeys as pilgrimages, crusades, or missions.

Pilgrimages

The art of pilgrimage is as old as recorded history. A pilgrimage is a journey, generally to a certain place, that is embarked upon for some sort of spiritual purpose. Many pilgrimages today are taken for the sake of discovering who we are … a very sacred quest. We long to reawaken our inner adventurer and psychic wanderer. For millennia there have been sacred sites to which people were drawn. Whether they went to Karnak in Egypt, Delphi in Greece or Angkor in Cambodia, humans have long embarked on journeys to discover themselves and the mystical within. They traveled lightly, relying solely on their intuition and soul's purpose. Today, millions of us still make pilgrimages. It is not necessary to go to the ends of the earth or to suffer physical hardship on the journey. It is not the destination that is magical, it is the act of traveling with all three of your eyes wide open. I know many people who have a sacred spot that they go to regularly to relax, commune with nature, and get intuitive messages. This spot, wherever it may be, is their pilgrimage place.

A Pilgrimage Place

Perhaps you already have a place you go to when you need to be spiritually recharged. It might be the family cabin, a park near your house, or an ocean boardwalk. If you don't, take a moment to sit quietly and visualize what your ideal pilgrimage place would look like. Would it be outside or a quiet spot in a temple? What would you hear? Inhale and ask yourself what scents you are picking up. Would there be other people there or would you be alone? Write down everything that you can think of that makes your sacred site so perfect for you. Keep that list and add to it when other thoughts arise. This list of elements can be incorporated into your home, your garden, or can help you decide where you want to go on vacation. It is one of the first steps in making each of life's journeys into a pilgrimage.

Quests

Like pilgrimages, people have embarked on quests since we started walking on two legs. A pilgrimage is a journey with a specific destination. Generally the person knows how to get to the destination, whether it is Mecca, Lourdes, or your family cabin. It is what occurs during and at the end of the pilgrimage that is unknown. A pilgrimage is destination-centered.

Conversely, a quest is a search for something that has an unknown location. You might expect to find something, like the Holy Grail, personal enlightenment, or the world's greatest purse, at the termination of it. However, quests are primarily journey-centered. Of greatest importance is the journey itself because that prepares you to receive unknown benefits. The term quest conjures up an image of a hero who overcomes great obstacles on a search for something that is missing in her life. Sometimes these quests last for years and take the searcher to exotic locations and cultures. Like a pilgrimage, however, your quest need not take you farther than your own neighborhood. The object of your quest is likely to be discovering yourself and your true nature. Your third eye will be your tool for discovering the Holy Grail of self-knowledge and mastery.

Elements of a Quest

Most of us spend a fair amount of time shopping and are familiar with how long it takes and how hard you sometimes have to work to find the perfect thing, whether it is a car or an outfit or a house. Psychic wanderers use that same method when they are on a quest, except their quest is likely to be about finding their life's purpose or understanding a particular relationship. Like a shopping excursion, though, quests have the same steps.

1) You have an idea of the type of thing you are looking for (a dress, a gift, a new vocation in life, a sense of peace).

2) Generally you have some idea of where you want to start looking (a car dealership, a flea market, Tikal, a meditation class).

3) You have a willingness to search as long as it takes to find what you are looking for. Your intention is to seek for as long and as hard as it takes.

4) You are open to looking in unexpected places if the first option doesn't work.

5) You trust that your intuition will tell you when you have found the exact, right thing. You will simply know.

You can use these elements of a quest whenever you are looking for something. They are just as valid in finding a new job as they are in finding a new way of living or carpeting for your living room. We all know people who have NO idea of what they are looking for or where to look. It is hard to get what you want if you don't have a clue as to what you are seeking. We also know people who give up as soon as they don't find something. Psychic wandering involves a commitment to keep wandering, looking, seeking, and listening to your intuition. You are flexible and able to change your journey if circumstances change. Finally, when you have found what you are looking for, you trust your intuitive wisdom about it.

Human beings were created to be explorers and adventurers. The urge to travel is in our genetic makeup. Not all of us can travel around the world, but all of us can live life as a spiritual journey. How to do that as a psychic wanderer is the focus of this book. My sister Jean and I will tell tales of our own journeys, both inward and outward, and give tips on how to make the journey joyful and done with effortless ease. Join us in becoming psychic wanderers and third eye travelers.

chapter two

If anyone points out the moon to you
and you see it, do you go on
staring at the finger?
—ANDREW HARVEY

Keep Your Third Eye and Mind Open

How to Open Your Third Eye

There are many ways to open your third eye and enhance your intuitive ability. Many of the methods come from ancient yogic practices and focus on breathing techniques. Watching our breath and merely focusing on the flow of breath is a very good way to enter into a type of trance. While the word trance sometimes has negative connotations, it really is simply a way to enter into a slightly altered state of consciousness. We all go in and out of trances all the time. Think of all the times you drive and arrive at your destination without much conscious awareness of anything that happened along the way. Remember what it is like to be in such a state of focus that the rest of the world fades out of awareness. These are both focus states or trances. It is very natural for us. What is perhaps a bit unnatural is intentionally entering into a trance on command. When we are in this state we are far more focused. We develop an awareness of things such as the sensations in our body, our emotions, our thoughts. When we can allow all of these things to enter into our awareness and yet not attach to any of them, we are in a state of trance. In this state of awareness we will receive intuitive information and see psychic visions.

Focusing on Your Tongue

In my experience, the quickest way to open my third eye and enter into this trance state is by focusing on and then relaxing my tongue. We constantly talk to ourselves, and when we do, we tend to move our tongues, just as if we were verbalizing out loud. If you concentrate on relaxing your tongue, you make it almost impossible for this sub-vocalization to occur. When you reduce your mental ruminating, you create room for your third eye to give you information. Take a break for a minute from reading this book and allow your jaw to loosen and your tongue to relax. Focus on your breath and let the tension melt from your jaw, face, and tongue. Then notice how very few thoughts you are experiencing when you don't move your tongue. You are in a very light and very useful state of trance.

Each person must find their own best way of relaxing their tongue. I imagine my tongue floating in my mouth while I let my chin drop slightly and my jaw loosen. Once you have mastered this technique, you can loosen your tongue in a matter of seconds. This exercise puts you into a very mild trance state in which your brainwaves are altered from high speed Beta waves to a slower Alpha state. In this altered consciousness, you are much more available to receive and understand intuitive messages. When I travel, I use this technique often. It gives me psychic information instantaneously while also helping me to relax. It is also quite effective when I am having difficulty sleeping.

Some people have told me they hate relaxing their tongue. They report having even more thoughts or tell me that all they can think about is whether they are loosening their tongue correctly. So, if this doesn't work for you, throw the suggestion away. You can find another way to open your third eye, perhaps by watching your breath or concentrating on a flame or other object. It doesn't matter what you use or how you do it, as long as it works for you. Loosening your tongue, however, is totally portable, can be done anywhere at any time, and no one needs to know you are doing it. My most memorable use of this technique was on a mountaintop in Peru.

Once, when I was in Machu Picchu, I was privileged to be able to enter the ruins at night. This is actually not allowed, but like so much in Latin America, a little cash closes a lot of eyes. I went with a group but soon decided that I was risking life and limb trying to climb slippery, steep stairs in darkness. So, I waited about halfway up while the rest of the group climbed higher. Left by myself, I sat quietly and let the magic and mystery of the ruins sink in to my soul. The ruins were totally dark, with no artificial light anywhere. I sat and marveled at the stars, realizing I never had a chance to really see them in the western world with our ambient lighting.

The sky was a gigantic jumble of beauty and I wished that I knew more about the constellations. With that knowledge, I thought, I would have been able to focus more on a particular formation and its message, rather than being overwhelmed by the sheer massiveness of the heavenly firmament.

Then I realized I was focusing on the knowledge and not on the message. I sat quietly, taking a few deep breaths, and let my tongue relax. Immediately, the ruins began to shimmer with a different type of energy. From out of the depth of the jungle far below, light began to dance, and a beautiful music rose within and around me. Above me, beams of light darted across the sky. I decided not to question where the lights were coming from, what they meant, or how I could be hearing music. I didn't care if the shooting lights above me were stars or flying saucers. For several hours, all I did was sit immersed in the beauty, awe, and mystery of that magical place. By opening my third eye and relaxing my need to define things, I had an experience beyond anything I can describe.

Live the Mystery

One aspect of opening your third eye is to learn that you don't need to understand everything. There are some things in life … like love and God and intuition … that defy explanation or scientific proof. Despite that, most of us have experienced all three. We may not be able to explain love, but we know it exists. We perhaps can't scientifically verify that intuition exists, but we can still use it to improve our lives. I believe things like God, ancient ruins, and love are not meant to be fully understood. Yet they are the very things that make living on this planet worthwhile.

I took a group to Greece a few years ago where we had a marvelous time touring the country and visiting many sacred and ancient sites. We were blessed to have a knowledgeable guide (Lily) who also was sympathetic to our interests. Once she learned that our group had metaphysical and spiritual leanings, she emphasized the ancient rituals and rites as well as discussing history and architecture.

At one point she shared with me how freeing it was to be able to talk openly to the group about such things. Most tour groups, she told me, only want to understand the how and why of the sites. They want to know how an ancient culture could build such massive structures and what the purpose was for the various buildings. Most of that information is simply unknown, but everyone seems to have a theory or a speculation, often stated as if it were a known fact.

Lily then said something that was perhaps my most profound learning of the trip. She said, "I don't really need to understand the mystery of these places. I would rather LIVE the mystery." I have traveled to many sacred sites. I have stood in awe before the pyramids of Egypt, marveled at the beauty of Angkor Wat, and been lost in the wonder of many Mayan ruins, and I agree with Lily. I would much prefer to live the mystery than to understand it.

Asking What and How Questions

On a recent trip to the Mayan ruins in Guatemala, I was part of a tour group of people who had no interest in spiritual things. I felt like an alien from Mars who was going around trying to feel energy while the rest of the group speculated on architecture and history. It was a very good reminder to me of why I love to travel with other spiritual seekers.

Our society trains us to ask why and when questions such as "Why did the Mayans build pyramids? When were these structures erected?" It is the scientific method, I suppose, that has been drilled into us since we were small. When you are psychically wandering, though, I have learned that the best questions to ask are what and how. Questions such as: "What can I learn about myself from this place?" or "How can I use what I am intuitively getting to improve my life?" One of the most important skills all intuitives should master is that of asking a good question. Many people are incredibly sloppy when they ask intuitive questions. When I do readings for people I am always asked questions such as "Why am I so unhappy?" or even "When am I going to die?" Almost always though, those answers are not what the person truly wants to know. The true desire behind the questions is, perhaps, something like, "What can I do to improve my enjoyment of life right now?" or, "How can I improve my physical health?"

It is really tempting to sit around asking "why?" but the truth is that it really doesn't matter. What matters is how and what. How can we thrive in uncertain times? What can we do to feel better in our bodies? How can we improve our relationships? What can I learn about myself by traveling?

It is frightening sometimes to have to ask a specific how or what question to your intuition. Crafting a good question feels a little like exposing ourselves. When we REALLY ask how to change something, we are already on the way to changing it. We have acknowledged that the issue exists and we have accepted the fact that we are the only ones who can change our lives.

Asking "why" questions keeps you stuck. Asking "how" questions frees you. Try this with any issue you might feel stuck on. Notice your thoughts and make note of how often you ask "why." Then, change your thoughts. Instead of asking, "Why am I in this situation?" ask instead, "How can I change, improve, or remove myself from this situation?" I am certain you will feel a sense of relief. Perhaps your intuition will not immediately give you an answer (although I suspect that it will give you something), but the very act of crafting a good question will make you feel more powerful and in control of the situation. Of course, there are many situations in which we are not in total control. We can, after all, only change ourselves. In even the most powerless of situations, though, there is a way to change or improve it. Asking yourself "how" is the first step.

It seems to me that the whys of some things are better left unknown. There is something humbling and spiritual about merely being in the mystery, without making up a storyline. I sometimes find myself being one of the story line makers, however. Not, of course, so much about the engineering of a site, but rather in the way of: "What past lives did I live here?" Perhaps, "Did aliens really help to move these huge blocks of stone?" Even, "Is that a portal I see up there in the stone face?" Ah yes, I am just as guilty as everyone else in wanting to understand and thus feel in control.

We all do this in our everyday surroundings as well. We want to know "Why does my husband act the way he does?" or "When will my job change?" These questions are as unanswerable as the mystery of how the stones were moved into place at Machu Picchu. One of my favorite Zen sayings is a line that goes something like this: "The Tao you can understand is not the real Tao." How true that is. I think I am fairly bright, but any God I could understand would be far too small to be worshiped. Truth be told, I don't understand much in my life. The internet is a mystery. I have no idea how my car works. I certainly have yet to figure out the banking system. Yet, I use and enjoy all these things. It is not necessary to understand something in order to enjoy it, learn from it and prosper because of using it.

I think that is at least part of why I travel. It takes me away from my environment where I can fool myself into thinking I understand and control things. It puts me in a frame of mind where I stop trying to understand the mystery and start living it.

Staying in the Now

One of the ways we get out of needing to control things is to stay in the moment and experience what is happening NOW. It seems easier to do when you are traveling, somehow, because everything usually is new to us. Jean tells about how she discovered this lesson:

> One of the greatest gifts my sister ever gave me was on a trip. We had just touched down in Cancun and were trying to arrange a taxi to our destination, a small village down the coast. I was tired and anxious, then it started to rain. I immediately went into my catastrophic poor-me mode, complaining about everything from my lack of preparation (I should have arranged the transport in advance, I thought) to the unfairness of rain during my Mexican getaway.
>
> Kathryn turned to me, calmly, although I am sure she wanted to throttle me, and said, "Jean, would you rather be in the minus 20-degree winter of Minnesota right now? What is so terrible about watching rain fall in paradise?"
>
> Of course she was right. It was not what was actually occurring that made me crazy, it was that my expectations

were of something else entirely. Expectations and rigidity will ruin any vacation.

Soon after Fred and I married back in the mid-1980s we booked a cruise. It was a combination of the honeymoon we'd never had and a much-needed mental health break. Even though money was more than tight, we were splurging. We were going to be gone over Valentine's Day, so I shopped for weeks for the perfect dress for that evening. I dieted, I waxed, I found the perfect shoes, I bought new lingerie. The whole point of the cruise became, for me, a perfect romantic evening.

I enjoyed the cruise but remained focused on this one evening and all the expectations I had of romance. It was as though I was going to star in a romantic chick flick. On Valentine's Day I woke up to the sound of my husband coughing…and coughing…and coughing. By evening he was too sick to even get up for dinner.

I wish I could say that I was a gracious nurse and loving wife. I was not. I was angry at the Universe and my spouse. I was not amused. I had a (hopefully quiet) temper tantrum. Just to show the Universe how upset I was, I refused to go to dinner on my own that night.

Honestly, I ruined a wonderful vacation by refusing joy. The night sky from the deck was still as beautiful, the breezes still as warm. I knew my husband adored me, but I would not recognize any of that. The world was awful because we could not have a candlelit dinner.

I do hope that I have changed, and that travel has helped me to do so. I try to acknowledge that the best made plans will go awry, and that I can only control my reactions…not the Universe.

*I am not saying I do not plan anymore! I am the god-
dess of planning and researching a trip. I spend hours on
the internet and the telephone securing reservations and
making connections. No guide book goes unread. Sometimes
I know far more that the tour guide about the site we are
trudging through. A great part of the joy of traveling, for
me, is the preparation and anticipation.*

*My husband, however, often barely knows what coun-
try we are going to visit. He has taken the Zen of travel to
new heights ... he just appears and accepts what each new
day brings. Our first couple of trips I spent many frustrat-
ing hours trying to include him in the planning, feeling hurt
and dismissed when his full cooperation just wasn't given.
Didn't he see how important I was? How necessary my
planning and worrying was to the success of the journey?
Why couldn't we share the joy of anticipation?*

*The answer? Because. Because he is much different from
me, and my planning drives him nuts. He does appreciate
having the plans made, tickets purchased and rental cars
waiting. He just does not enjoy doing it. I do. Our deal is that
I will plan, he will appreciate. He cannot whine or blame me
if things fall apart since he did not help prepare. I have let go
of the expectation of sharing planning bliss ... it will never
happen.*

*Travel can be the most rewarding meditation, a true time
of living in the moment and connecting with the soul. Conversely, one can fill the vacation days with so much concern
and worry over having enough fun that one might as well
have stayed in the office. What makes the difference? Largely
attitude. Attitude and the knowledge that a vacation can be a
holy experience. It is easy nowadays to visit an ashram to sit
in meditation, a monastery to walk the maze in silent prayer,*

or to join with several hundred others in an intimate experience with a new age leader at a Mayan temple. All of these pilgrimages are worthy and will bring their own rewards. I do not mean to disparage or discourage anyone from using their two weeks of vacation in these pursuits, but they are not the only way to find spirit while traveling. We all hold within us the intrinsic knowledge of what we need to find each day to truly thrive. One gift of travel is that it gives us the time and space to listen to that internal knowing. The teacher will come if we are open and listen.

Although I prefer more adventurous travel, enlightenment could come at Disney World as well as in Tibet. Washing the dishes can be as sacred an act as offering incense. Spirit can speak to one on the "It's a Small World" ride or through a flower growing out of a rock on the mountain in Nepal. The key is in listening and looking, in opening the eyes and heart to the sacred.

*Every-day magic! This cat took up residence
in a Spirit House in Cambodia.*

Although these lessons come more easily, in my opinion, on a journey, they also are found in our day-to-day life. Each and every day we receive messages … IF we are willing to hear it.

Jean had this experience: *I drove along a straight-as-an-arrow country road on my way to a work appointment. A dense fog had settled over the early spring landscape and there seemed to be just a small bubble of clarity around the car before the world disappeared into a shroud of gray mist. Going very slowly on the unfamiliar road, I glanced at a young pine tree twenty feet from the road. On the very top of the small tree was a bald eagle. I slammed on the brakes and gingerly eased the car back and onto the narrow gravel shoulder. Quietly I inched out of the driver's seat and walked on the gravel shoulder back to the tree. The magnificent bird looked down on me with seeming curiosity and vocalized. The fog suddenly seemed denser, sound was muffled and magnified at the same time; the eagle and I seemed to be alone on the planet.*

Out of the stillness came a beating of wings, and from nowhere appeared another eagle. She perched on the top of the small pine, causing it to bend under her weight and forcing her spouse into an undignified burst of activity to regain his balance. Just then a semi truck full of cows going to market noisily veered around me, horn blaring—the moment was lost as the birds took flight.

I touched the divine in those few moments. For a minute that lasted an eternity I was out of place and time, out of the mundane and dwelling in a land where all is one; where an eagle is god and I was goddess and the fog embodied mystery and grace and holiness.

That stillness, that rightness, that temple is within me forever. The fog had swallowed the future road ahead, the past was invisible, even paths to the sides of me were unknowable. There was just the moment, and the silence, and the communion. It was everything.

When I had left home that morning I had not expected to be touched by the sacred. I was rushed, worried about driving in the dense fog, irritated that I wouldn't be able to enjoy the scenery of Northern Minnesota. Yet, a great gift was given to me. I was given something I needed and yet could not have imagined.

That is the wonder of spirit and travel. Because we look at new places with fresh eyes we can really see what is there. The spirit that resides in every atom and particle can reveal itself more easily to our intensely focused eyes. Jean could have easily missed her communion with the eagles by simply not seeing them. Instead, the Universe gave her a gift. One very useful exercise you can do anywhere is to look at ordinary surroundings with the fresh new eyes we sometimes only use on vacation.

Seeing your home with fresh eyes exercise

Imagine seeing your home for the first time. Pretend that you are from a different culture, totally unacquainted with modern American life. Would you more clearly see that the fresh flowers and candles on the dinner table are an offering of thanksgiving and a supplication for health? Is that an altar to the deceased there on the piano, with all the ancestors' photos so carefully arranged? Surely the prolonged purification ceremonies and creams must form an important part of the religious habits of the occupants of the home? Look at the huge and expensive bathing rooms set aside only for the cleansing rituals.

In all seriousness, try to see your home through the eyes of a psychic wanderer. See the care with which you have chosen your belongings and their placement in your home. Notice the everyday rituals you perform and try to see beneath them to their true significance. That fifteen-minute shower every morning is about much more than cleanliness. It may be your only time alone during the day, a time of meditation and sensuality. Perhaps it is your moment to feel the caress of Mother Earth's waters nourishing your body and soul.

Our Dutch cousins recently spent several weeks in the USA, and their request was always "show us the REAL America." Seeing our state through their eyes was wonderful. My favorite moment was on a tour of Split Rock Lighthouse. The three of us were part of a group of twenty-five people dutifully following the park ranger from site to site. I noticed my cousin stepping aside from the crowd and taking a photo of the group's feet. With his traveler's eyes he had noticed that every single person had on white athletic shoes. We all laughed. None of the rest of us would ever have said that it was an American trait to wear comfortable shoes!

Wherever we are, wise persons through the ages have taught us the key to spirituality and growth is being present, being in the moment … and realizing that each moment is sacred. When we remove ourselves from the familiar and *make a conscious and deliberate choice to see the world not only as tourists but also as pilgrims; when we take the time away from our mind numbingly familiar routines; when we stretch and challenge ourselves to relate to and understand other cultures...that is when we can see the sacredness of our everyday life.*

chapter three

The more I traveled the more I realized
that fear makes strangers of
people who should be friends.

—SHIRLEY MACLAINE

Lessons from Strangers on the Path

Some of the greatest joys and challenges of all adventures come from the people we meet along the way. In our day-to-day life we become very homogenized in our encounters. For most of us, at least, the people we meet and relate with look, act, speak, and think very much like we do. Because of that, we don't really need to pay much intuitive attention to them. We know, without really thinking about it, exactly what our husbands will eat for breakfast, the likely conversation around the water cooler at work and the topic of the small talk with the cashier at the grocery store. If asked, it is unlikely that we could recall or even have noticed what our coworkers wore that day or what the main conversation was around the dinner table. There is nothing wrong with this, as a certain level of predictability and constancy is very comforting, but it does nothing to encourage you to live life with your third eye open.

During your psychic wanderings though, you must be attentive and alert. In foreign countries, everything is slightly different from that with which we are familiar. One of the things that surprises me each journey is how many ways it is possible to flush a toilet. I always seem to need to take a few minutes each time just to figure out exactly where the button, lever, or other flush mechanism has been hidden. That is a small example, of course, but life and learning are made up of small things.

My most delightful toilet discovery was in a hotel in Istanbul, Turkey. It was a public toilet in the lobby of our hotel and it had the most wonderful buttons you could push. One button played bird songs to cover up the sounds you might make. Another button released a burst of air freshener. A third actually warmed the toilet seat. I was merrily bending over the toilet playing with the buttons to see what each did when I hit the fourth and last button and was rewarded with a spray of warm water all over my face. Apparently you are supposed to be sitting DOWN when you hit the bidet button.

Usually, though, it is not the different currency or language or flush mechanism that gets the attention of our third eye. Rather, it is an encounter with a person that turns out to be completely unexpected and usually, but not always, delightful.

In our everyday lives, most of us encounter strangers on a daily basis. We pass dozens of people each day on the streets, in stores, perhaps through our work. It is so common, in fact, that we have usually quit even noticing them. We can go to a busy mall or event and walk by hundreds of people without giving them a glance or having any recall of who we passed.

Being in an unfamiliar locale, though, often prompts us to notice people we would not necessarily have noticed on our home turf. If we pay attention, our intuition and third eye will often use them to give us messages or to make a point.

Many years ago I was on vacation with my family on Mexico's Yucatan peninsula. One day we left the beach to visit the ancient Mayan ruin of Coba. Unlike the more popular ruins of Chichen Itza and Tulum, Coba is mostly not excavated and, therefore, not heavily visited. We were among only a handful of tourists in the entire area. Narrow jungle roads separated the excavated sites from one another. We walked toward one of the sites down a path at least a half mile long, meeting no one along the way and hearing no sounds except the birds and other rustling jungle noises. Finally reaching the site, we spent about a half hour thoroughly exploring the ruins. Our group of five (my husband, Loren, my sister, Jean, and her husband, Fred, and my brother, Jim) rejoiced in having the area completely to ourselves. Finally, we left to visit another site, returning on the same and only pathway. We walked slowly, looking for toucans and admiring the large trees that surrounded us.

Suddenly, a stranger who seemed to come out of nowhere joined us. Our new addition was indeed a strange person. He was tall and gangly and wore unusually colorful and baggy pants, and a shirt with puffy sleeves. His clothes and demeanor made him look like a cross between a circus clown and a medieval troubadour. His wild red hair hadn't seen a comb for a long time. He joined our party, falling in step with my brother Jim, nodding and saying hello in a heavily accented voice. We were all rather shaken and uncomfortable. There had been no one else at the ruins we had just visited and no other way in or out except by this path. He seemed to have appeared out of thin air.

We walked together for a short time in what was now an awkward silence. None of us felt comfortable with our new friend, yet we weren't sure what to do. Finally, my sister and I stopped to admire a large spider web. Our friend stopped too. We waited. He waited. Then, perhaps sensing his lack of welcome, he left our group and walked on in front of us. As he walked away, we all noticed that he was carrying something in his right hand, but none of us could say what it was. He held it out admiringly in front of him as he walked. It seemed to be a cylindrical object of some kind, which glowed as the sun struck it. My third eye buzzed, sensing energy waves emanating from it. Feeling freed, we followed him at a distance of less than 200 feet. At one point the path made a turn and we lost sight of him for a few minutes. By the time we made the turn, he had disappeared.

Then began the speculation about our visitor. My husband, as down-to-earth and logical as they come, declared him to be a German tourist with poor taste in clothes and a severe drug problem. He explained the man's sudden appearance by saying that he could have been asleep hidden in the ruins, and awakened after we left to follow us. Then, my husband explained, he must have left the path at the turn to hide in the jungle or make his own path to another site.

My intuition did not buy that theory at all. I declared, only half jokingly, that he was a visitor from outer space, materializing to join us for a few minutes and then using the magical device he held in his hand to transport himself elsewhere. Our group laughingly enjoyed the speculation as we walked to the next site.

The last ruin we saw at Coba was the pyramid. There we finally ran into a crowd, a busload of tourists who stood photographing the structure and, on a bench by himself, sat the man I now thought of as Starman. He looked up at us and nodded. Speculation continued as we walked to the gate. How had he beaten us to the pyramid without ever reappearing on the path? Leaving him napping on the bench, still holding his crystalline object, we picked up our car in the parking lot, where only our car and the tour bus remained. We then drove several miles down the road, stopping at a tiny town to have lunch. We sat at a table in an outdoor café. As we finished our meals, we were shocked to see Starman once again. He was walking down the highway toward Coba—coming from the opposite direction of where we had seen him last.

We had left him a half hour before, sitting at a pyramid in a ruin at least five miles away. It was impossible for him to have walked that far in that amount of time, yet there was no sign of any companion or a vehicle. Even my logical husband was having a hard time coming up with an explanation, although hitchhiking was his final conclusion. Why though, if he hitchhiked away from Coba, was he now walking toward it? Who gave him the ride? The tour bus?

I will never know, of course, who or what Starman was. I only know that the world is full of unexplained phenomena. Being a psychic wanderer allows for these types of encounters. Meeting Starman opened all of our third eyes. We had a lively discussion about the possibilities and it seemed to challenge us all to look at things more clearly and vividly than we had before.

There is no reason, of course, that Starman could not just as easily have appeared in my local grocery store. Perhaps he has. The likelihood of my noticing or paying attention would be a great deal less though, than on a jungle path. When I shop in my local neighborhood I am on a mission (mostly to get in and out as quickly as possible). I would likely have passed by a strange man like Starman without a second glance. In contrast, as adventurers at a Mayan ruin, our senses were alert, we were willing to look for signs, and we were more likely to trust our intuition to give us an explanation. Well, at least I was. Loren still sticks with the German hippy version.

The Starman story illustrates several important principles of psychic wandering. First, when you are out of your element you tend to notice things you would otherwise walk right past. One of the things I love to look at when I travel is doors. I have dozens of photographs of colorful and unique doors in my travel photo albums. At home, though, I walk past many interesting doors without a glance in their direction. The doors are the same; it is ME who is different. Would I have paid attention to Starman if he had walked near me at a local fair or in the aisles of Costco? Probably not.

Another advantage of psychic wandering is that you have the time and leisure to contemplate your experiences. In the case of the Starman sighting, I was with a family group. By discussing what happened at length we had a lively conversation and varied interpretations. In the end, we all defined the experience slightly differently, depending on our world view. As a mystic and psychic, I had no difficulty interpreting our encounter as one of the third kind. As a lawyer and pragmatist, my husband found a completely rational explanation for what happened. The rest of my family fell somewhere in between him and me in their understanding.

On any adventure, it is wise to leave your preconceived expectations behind. Pack an open mind and use it freely. I will never know who or what Starman was. It doesn't matter. That day opened my mind to the knowledge that all things are possible ... even a materializing and dematerializing person from another dimension.

Getting Intuitive Information from Strangers Exercise

Here is an exercise you can use anywhere that will allow you to ask for and receive intuitive messages from the strangers you meet. When you wake in the morning, take a few minutes to set the intention that you will see a stranger sometime during the day and that you will get an intuitive message from that person. You don't need to worry about how that will happen, just keep your third eye open and notice intuitively when someone just seems to jump out at you.

When you see him or her (and you will know when you do), ask yourselves these questions:

1) How would I describe this person? Use as many descriptive phrases as you can. Don't just use a physical description, i.e. brown hair, tall, well dressed. Also use descriptive words such as sophisticated, rebellious, mysterious, and so forth.

2) What is this person doing? For example, is she fidgeting as she waits, or is he intensely focused? Is she carrying anything or doing an activity? If so, what?

3) What would this person say to me if we spoke? It is possible that the person may, in fact, speak to you. In that case, of course, just remember what was said. However, if the person you are intuitively drawn to does not speak to you or even notice you, just ask your intuition what this person would say to you if they had the chance and inclination.

If possible, write down the answers to these three questions. Be as descriptive and imaginative as possible.

The trickiest part of teaching intuitive practices is teaching people to interpret their messages. The key to interpretation is often hidden in the way that you describe the intuitive experience. So, the more descriptive and colorful words you use, the better the interpretation.

Here is the way to interpret what your stranger is saying to you:

1) The words you used to describe your stranger will describe YOU as you are right now. Of course, the physical description will not be the same (your person might even be of the opposite sex) but the words will have meaning. For example, perhaps you are a young man and yet your stranger was an old, homeless woman. Some of your descriptive words could be, "tired, shabby, poor, etc." These words will, in some way, describe how you are FEELING that day.

2) The words to describe what the person is doing are your intuition giving you advice about what YOU should do that day. In the above example, perhaps the old woman was rummaging in a trash can. The young

man might interpret that as advice to look for some-thing (a job ... a girlfriend ... a new car) in a place he would never bother to look or that he feels is beneath him.

3) Finally, the words of advice your stranger gives you are just that ... your intuition is giving you advice for the day. In my example, perhaps the woman might say, "Get away!" In that case, the advice to the young man would be that he should get away in some fashion that day.

Sometimes the people you meet along the way seem to be there strictly to teach you a lesson that you might not have been able to learn in any other way. It is as if you have pre-arranged with that soul, perhaps in another lifetime, to meet you for a short time, teach you something or aid you in some fashion, and then be on their way. You can use this exercise any time and with any question. I have asked strangers for intui-tive advice in Turkey and at Walmart. It is not the exotic locale that makes the advice special. Rather, it is using your intuition to find the right person, asking the questions, paying attention and then intending to get and accept the message.

I seem to meet a lot of strangers on jungle paths. A few years ago in Costa Rica I was hiking with some friends on a vine-covered path. We were bird watching and my eyes were on the trees, looking for birds, NOT on the ground looking for spiders. I promise you, I never look for spiders. You see, I am not afraid of a lot anymore, but spiders are definitely not on my list of things I wish to see or experience. So, I sup-pose, it is not surprising that they keep showing up for me to notice them.

On that day, a huge tarantula crossed the path directly in front of me and then, for some inexplicable reason, decided to stop and just sit there, blocking my way. I froze. He froze. Neither of us, apparently, was ever going to move again. Despite the urging of my friends saying that I could go around him, I was not about to make a move nearer to the thing. We were at a standoff.

Although the path was quite remote and untraveled, a man suddenly came up from behind me. He was dressed very strangely for a jungle path, wearing a suit and tie. As he walked up, he said something to the effect of: "Face your fear and you won't ever feel it that strongly again."

Frankly, I was annoyed. This was a spider, for Pete's sake. Not just any spider either, but a really, really BIG spider. Somehow, though, being a coward in front of my friends was something I could handle, while being fearful in front of this arrogant stranger was more than I could bear. I took a big deep breath and walked past my nemesis … and survived. I have no idea how the spider did.

The stranger walked with me for a while after that, lecturing me on fear. Then, in a way that I suppose I should be getting used to, he turned a corner and disappeared.

Like Starman, I will never know who my self-appointed psychiatrist was or why he appeared and disappeared. From that day though, I am not nearly as afraid of spiders, although trust me, I still do NOT like them. Just recently in Panama yet another tarantula crossed my path (yes, I do seem to have a karmic thing with crossing tarantulas), and I was able to just stop and watch it without my heart pounding … much.

Another thing I don't like is snakes. Which, since I live in Minnesota and we have very few snakes, does not really make much sense. Still, ever since I was a small child, even the idea of a snake or seeing a picture of one in a magazine or on television would fill me with horror. Maybe it is a past-life thing. Maybe I just don't like snakes.

One thing I have learned though is that what we fear seems to always appear in our lives. Not long ago I was in Mexico, touring the Copper Canyon. It is an amazing place. The canyon itself is said to be five times as large as our Grand Canyon. It is stunning.

I was taking a hike with a few friends and was admiring the view of the canyon. They decided to hike on and I wanted to sit alone and just meditate and enjoy the beauty and quiet. I went out on a ledge and sat, inhaling the solitude of a perfectly quiet and sunny day. I asked for a sign about what I should do next in my life. Then, after sitting for a bit and luxuriating in the serenity, I headed back to the lodge where we were staying.

As I walked along the path, I heard a slight rustling sound. Expecting to perhaps see a squirrel or some other small animal, I looked down and there it was. The biggest darn snake in the world.

OK, I am prone to exaggeration, but this snake really was at least as long than I am tall and he was heading MY way. Nothing in my experience had taught me what to do when meeting a snake of amazing size. So, I just kept walking and we passed by each other on the path. I think we might even have nodded to each other.

This is not a particularly amazing story, except for this. I didn't scream. I didn't freeze. I realized I was not even terribly afraid. It turns out snakes are really not all that scary.

So, I think my friend the snake was the sign I had requested in my meditation. These are scary times and yet, when we finally meet the thing that scares us the most, often all it does is just slide on past.

There is a wonderful Buddhist teaching that says, "When the student is ready, the teacher will appear." The same thing, I think, is true for lessons like my spider and snake phobias. When you're ready, your counselor, guide, or psychiatrist will show up. When you are ready to face your fear, it is likely to just slide painlessly past you.

Remove yourself from familiarity

To meet that guide though, you need to remove yourself from the familiarity of your day-to-day life. You don't need to go to the jungle, but you do need to leave your house. I suppose it is possible that the teacher might just knock on your door, but I think that is pushing your luck. When you are prepared to learn a lesson, set the intent that the teacher will appear. Then, put yourself in unfamiliar surroundings. If you can't travel abroad, you can certainly go to a different store than usual or walk a different route to work. If you are feeling the nudge of Spirit that says you are about to learn a lesson, put yourself in a new place for a week and wait. The teacher or psychiatrist will come to find you.

Sometimes, all it takes is an ability to see the extraordinary in our day-to-day lives. Jean tells this story of an encounter in her local supermarket that changed the whole way she viewed life. All she had to do was go shopping. As she tells it:

It was cold, numbingly cold, a cold that only a Minnesotan in January can truly understand. I was not going to the tropics anytime soon—this winter our money was all going into a new roof. I had a bad cold and a bad case of cabin fever. Believe me, the last thing I wanted to do was go grocery shopping. But we were out of coffee, and a January morning without coffee is simply not acceptable.

Ten minutes later the boots, scarves, hat, mittens, and parka were finally on. I slipped and slid down the back sidewalk to climb into my complaining car and head to the Rainbow Foods a mile from my house. At that moment I truly thought I was the most miserable person in the world. Falling on my butt as I entered the store door reaffirmed my assessment.

All I could think about as I filled my cart with routine purchases was that I could not travel this winter, I was stuck in my horrible neighborhood where nothing ever happened, in horrible Minnesota in the horrible USA. NOTHING good could come of this day. Then I turned into the toilet paper aisle, and there were four Tibetan monks in their red robes. They even wore sandals on their brown feet! I must admit I stopped dead in my tracks and stared. I am sure my mouth dropped open. They were laughing hysterically and examining each and every type of tissue that was on display, passing the packages back and forth to each other and commenting.

They saw me there and pantomimed a welcome, so soon I was trying to pick out my Charmin while bowing and attempting to shake their hands. An interpreter soon joined us with his arms full of cat food. These monks were visiting from Dharamsala, India, where they lived in exile from Tibet. They were helping my neighborhood establish a temple and meditation center nearby.

The interpreter said that their favorite activity was going to the grocery store. The monks found all of the colors and choices to be intoxicating; they could lose themselves for hours wandering the aisles. They also found great pleasure in the complexity of the American mind ... that we could care so very much to make the perfect choice to wipe our bottoms but not find time to meditate or practice religion.

There seemed to be no judgment at all in that statement, just a wonderment that humans could be so blessed and so different. "Perhaps," said one monk, "the choosing of the toothpaste or toilet paper was the meditation?"

In the months that followed I would often see my four friends, interpreter beside them, sitting in the coffee shop bakery of the store. Always they would incline their heads and smile, often nudging each other or pointing at me. I think that they would sit for hours at that coffee shop, making their daily tea last the entire time, just watching the Americans hurry by, always with smiles on their faces.

This chance meeting with four travelers taught me more than any trip to an exotic locale ever could. Each time I shop now, and find myself anxious or rushed, I remember that even grocery shopping can be a spiritual act. I learned that day that we are blessed beyond belief to have a choice, to have abundance, to have modern complexity and that I can make each of the thousand choices I make each day matter.

As Jean learned by that encounter, seeing our mundane lives through fresh eyes can be a spiritual practice. Using our third eyes to view our day-to-day lives makes each experience take on the excitement of world travel. After all, our lives ARE exotic when viewed from an outsider's eyes.

Sometimes we forget that when we travel WE seem very exotic to the locals. We have heard so much about the ugly American syndrome that we don't always appreciate how people in other countries are fascinated by our foreignness and want to talk to us. In almost every country I have visited people have come up to me, eager to practice English and to learn about America. In some countries, China particularly, I have had people walk up to me, touch my clothing as if in amazement at what I am wearing. To them (at least fifteen years ago) my style of dressing was as unique as the monk's red robes are to us.

As Jean tells it: *"In Kathmandu Fred and I had been running for several days, taking in every temple and ghat, busing and hiking up into the Himalayas to see the countryside, even taking a brilliant morning flight over Everest. There was only one day left in Nepal, and several monuments and temples yet to see.*

Instead, we took the bus from our hotel to a local market and just wandered. There were few tourists there, and we enjoyed the break from the street vendors and constant noise. When a sudden cloudburst came we rushed into a doorway for shelter. A mother and her little girl were scurrying past, and the three-year-old fell off the stone sidewalk into the path of the heavy traffic. Without hesitation I reached out and picked her up from the gutter, stepping back into the shelter with her.

The look of joy and amazement on both the young mother's and the little girl's faces were priceless. It was, I think, as if a fairy had suddenly appeared and picked her up. I handed her to her mother, who joined us in the shelter and shyly pointed to her daughter and said her name. We all pantomimed a conversation for a few minutes, the rain stopped, and with much Namaste-ing we parted.

It remains a favorite moment of mine from a favorite trip. It also changed how I perceive myself when I travel. Up to this point I had tried to blend in and not be a tourist (as though I was ever going to be thought to be a local in Kathmandu). Through this brief meeting I learned that I was one of the "Strangers on the Road" of life for those in the countries I passed through. I can be a positive encounter and an ambassador for my country. I like to think that little girl in Nepal remembers and feels special when she thinks of the experience.

Dare yourself to experience life to its fullest when you travel. Sometimes that may mean a contrary choice; skip the included tour to the fifteenth cathedral of the day and sit at a café with a glass of wine. Allow yourself to do what you want in the moment, to have Spirit lead you to what you need.

Instead of rushing around the bazaar in Istanbul Fred and I sat and had coffee in a sunlit café right outside. At the table next to us were several beautiful teenage girls, all wearing heavy makeup and trendy clothing, smoking and enjoying the day. One of the girls worked up the courage to speak to us in very broken English. "Are you from London?" she asked. When we told her we were from the United States, the girls pulled their chairs and beverages over to our table and chatted away.

Worshiping in Kathmandu.

They were from Saudi Arabia, here for the summer on vacation. They loved the U.S. and everything American. "Please, tell us all about what it is like there," they begged. "Can you drive?" "Do you work?" "Can you go to a night club with your husband?"

I asked a few questions back and was shocked by the answers. The girls were enjoying their few weeks of freedom but were going back to the hijab, dress restrictions, and chaperones when they returned home. There was a palpable longing for freedom and education. They all commented that they would soon be married and their lives would be over. I would never exchange that conversation and chance to better understand the longing of those young Saudi women for all the gold in the bazaar!

Similarly, I had a conversation with a young man in China that completely opened my eyes to how people from the United States are viewed. After introductions, he asked, "Is it true that Americans can own guns?" I said yes. He continued, "Have you ever SEEN a gun?" When I said yes, he got excited. "Have you ever held one?" Again, I responded yes. Wide-eyed, he said, "Have you ever shot one?" Rather sheepishly, I had to admit that I had. "Oh, my," he sighed. "I would love to see one someday."

It was then that I realized that owning, using, or even seeing a gun was against the law in China. Actually, I am not at ALL opposed to that but it truly opened my eyes to how exotic and strange we are to other nationalities. It also taught me that it is a small world and what we say or do has a profound influence, no matter where we are.

A few years ago some cousins from the Netherlands came to visit the United States, staying with me for two weeks. Carla and Martin are seasoned psychic wanderers, although I doubt they would ever use that phrase. They have just the right enthusiasm and joy to view even simple journeys as an adventure.

Martin came to Minnesota looking for the *real* America. He had previously visited New York and California but was convinced that America was more than skyscrapers and Hollywood. He wanted to see how we really lived.

Like Jean's story of the Buddhist monks, Carla and Martin viewed every new experience as a lesson. They much preferred to go to a grocery store than the Mall of America or a concert in the park to a concert at Orchestra Hall. They took great joy in their visit to meet a banker, asking me later why everyone always asked how they were. Did they look sick?

Everywhere we went we heard Martin's cry, "Carla, Carla, this is the REAL America!"

All of us have experienced the joy that comes from taking a small child to see something for the first time. Because we are with them, we, too, see and experience the place with fresh, new eyes. Psychic wandering is like that. By using our psychic eyes, we see beyond the veil of ordinary perception. We see the beauty in myriad varieties of toilet paper. We can ponder the differences in how different cultures do their banking or cooking. Maybe we even wonder how we really are.

These types of experiences can be had in every city and town in the world. Psychic wandering is about the joy of the experience of looking for the different, the unseen or unnoticed that lurks just out of sight of our ordinary senses. It is, however, there to be viewed by our soul and our third eye.

chapter four

In moments of great uncertainty
on my travels, I have always felt that
something is protecting me,
that I will come to no harm.

—TAHIR SHAH

Always Travel with Protection

Of course, we don't always want to walk around with our third eye wide open. There are many times when I find that I don't want to know what other people are feeling or thinking or when I simply want to enjoy the scenery and forget everything else. Like all things psychic, the key to using our third eye is to use it intentionally. We are in control of when we want to see with our psychic vision. We make the decision when to use it and when we merely wish to use our other five senses.

Because most people don't even believe they have intuitive ability, they don't use it, of course. Once we have discovered what a valuable tool it is, though, we want to be able to use it when we want but also to turn it off when we don't wish to use it. It is a skill like any other ability that gets better with practice and needs to be nurtured to be mastered.

Traveling gives us a perfect opportunity to practice our psychic skills. Because we are outside of our element and natural environment, our eyes (all three of them) tend to be more open to seeing things from a fresh perspective. Even then, though, the one thing that will quickly shut our third eye down is to view things from a state of judgment. When we are judging things we are using our conscious mind and we will generally see and get what we expect...NOT what we are actually getting psychically.

A few years ago Jean and I were on a photo safari in Kenya, Africa. Everyone who goes on these safaris longs to see the big five—elephants, rhinos, leopards, buffaloes, and, of course, lions. After several days on safari, we had seen an amazing variety of animals, but we had yet to see the king of the beasts. On our last day of the safari, we were all a little anxious that we would go home without a lion sighting. Jean and I decided we would do everything in our power, both physically and psychically, to see a lion on that last day. We had read about how lions could be spooked by loud talking, noises, and even bright colors. So, when we headed out that morning we were wearing neutral colors, shushing our companions, and trying to create the perfect environment for the lions to appear. We were, in fact, judging our travel mates, annoyed by their chatter and bright clothing and sure they were going to destroy our chance to see our lion and satisfy our goal. We had left that quiet intuitive space of calm where intentions are set, and had entered into a space of judgment.

Then, we came upon a gathering of safari vehicles. In the Samburu National Reserve, as in many game reserves, a lion sighting will be radioed from one jeep to another and the vehicles converge quickly, driving fast, making noise and raising dust. Jean and I were annoyed. It was all very different from what we thought should happen for a proper lion sighting.

Apparently though, the lions hadn't read the same article we had read. The pride barely looked up to notice the converging traffic jam. As we craned our necks to see over the crowd, one huge lion looked up and walked toward our vehicle, lying down to take advantage of the shade our Range Rover was casting. In the midst of all the noise and commotion, he took a nap, just a few feet from our amazed eyes.

These wild lions rested in the shadow of our jeeps, totally unconcerned about us.

Lions, apparently, are a lot like psychic information. They don't always come on command or act the way we expect them to act. All of our judgment of other people had caused both Jean and me to be cranky and out of sorts all morning... and it almost caused us to miss what we had gone to Kenya to see.

Judgment exercise

All judgments start with the language that we use. In intuitive practices, it is very important to use language that truly says what you mean. In this exercise, start by just observing some of the words you use on a daily basis, such as bad, good, right, wrong, fair, unfair, should, shouldn't and so forth. In one way or another, all these words imply a judgment. You don't need to do anything about the words, at this point, just notice how big a part they are in your life. Bring your attention to your thoughts and judgments when you are doing simple activities such as eating. Notice the thoughts you have about the food as you eat it. Don't try to analyze or change your judgments, just notice that they are there. If possible, ask yourself one thing. Does this judgment enhance my life? Most of the time, the answer will be no. Your food is not really bad for you. You might, however, feel better if you ate something different. Use your intuition to help you make choices without labeling those choices. The more you eliminate judgment from your life, the more room your intuition has to gently whisper advice to you. If you want to live a less judgmental life, you must first become aware of your own automatic thoughts and judgments. Learning to think non-judgmentally takes practice. Don't judge yourself for judging. Just slowly, gradually, one thought at a time, tame the burden of labeling everything as good or bad and just accept things for what they are.

Judgment will quite often keep us from getting messages, and it certainly doesn't only happen in the wilds of Africa. Years ago I was on a city bus on my way to work when a very ragged and dirty man sat down beside me. I immediately went into a judgment mode, noticing only his rather unpleasant odor and dirty fingernails. My mind created a story about him, thinking he was likely homeless and possibly dangerous. My body tensed and I clasped my belongings to me tightly.

As we sat in uncomfortable silence next to each other, he turned to me, smiled, and said, "You have really beautiful eyes." Then, he stood up and got off at the next stop.

I left the bus feeling both honored and ashamed. He had given me a gift when all I had given him was judgment. My judgment about him had shut down my third eye so that I could not see the blessing that he was going to give me. Gifts come in the most unusual wrapping sometimes … if our judgments allow us to open them.

The key to remote viewing

When I teach my students remote viewing (the intuitive art of seeing beyond your normal vision by using your psychic gifts), the first lesson is to remove all judgment about what they are viewing. They are instructed to sit quietly, loosen their tongue and jaw, and focus on their target (what they are attempting to see intuitively). Then they are told to receive whatever information, image, or sensation they get in their mind's eye, without labeling it.

Most people have a difficult time not labeling what they see with their third eye. To teach this skill, I usually put a photograph in an envelope and ask the students to draw the photograph without seeing it with their physical eyes, but rather using their mind's eye. I instruct them to just draw the shapes, colors, or other things they see with their psychic vision, but NOT to label or define to themselves what they are drawing.

Despite these instructions, the students tend to draw pictures, rather than shapes. A round circle might become a wheel…or a sun. A square could be a house or a field. In remote viewing, this labeling gets in the way. Often we can find elements of the target in their drawing (e.g. a square or red or dots) only after we take away the extra things they added to have the drawing look like something familiar.

As in remote viewing, it is important in life not to label or judge what you get intuitively. Accept the sensation that comes to you, attempt not to label it, and then let your intuition guide you as to the meaning.

How to shut your third eye

Sometimes, though, what you really want is to intentionally shut your third eye. I do this when I don't want information to come at me indiscriminately. Common places for me to shut my third eye are airports, hospitals, large events and shopping malls. These places can be information-overload centers for a person with an open third eye. If you have ever left a busy party or a crowded supermarket feeling exhausted, you know that feeling.

I was in an airport very early one morning when I felt a very strong desire for a drink, followed by the smell of alcohol. As I always do when hit out of the blue with strong desires or emotions, I asked, "Is this mine?" I immediately knew that this was not my urge. Looking up, I saw a woman who seemed very harried and upset. I was certain I was psychically picking up on her desire, although I did not, of course, ask her. Once I asked myself that question, the urge and uncomfortableness I was feeling went away and I no longer could smell the scent. It was not necessary for me to know that information about her and did neither of us any good.

Ask: Is this mine?

So, one way you can shut down your third eye is to set your intention that you will only receive information and sensations that have to do with YOU. It does you no good to go into a grocery store and "know" that the cashier just had a fight with her husband. You don't need to feel the fear or anger of the person next to you on the airplane. If you feel an unexplainable emotion or physical reaction (headache, tension, pain, or discomfort), always ask: "Is this mine?" If it is not yours, the sensation will disappear as quickly as it came. If it is yours, you can then ask: "What message does this sensation have for me?"

All psychics (well, at least all sane psychics) must learn to shield themselves from energy that is not theirs. They also need to figure out when the information they get is about them…and when it is not. Here, Jean describes a few instances where she received emotional "feelings" that were not hers and her methods for dealing with them.

> I was sixteen and on a two-week road trip with my parents. Does anything else need to be said about my state of mind? Everything was largely boring and certainly far beneath my adolescent approval.
>
> One of our last stops was Gettysburg and I was advocating for skipping it and getting home a day earlier. As we got closer I had announced that I would wait in the car and read. Luckily, the day was scorchingly hot and I opted to get out at the first stop.

As we walked out onto the first site every ounce of my body reacted. It was one of my first experiences with feeling the emotions of a site. The soil itself seemed to emanate sorrow.

As we slowly drove and walked through the battlefields I recognized places even though I had never been there before, particularly an old house that stood amidst the battlefields. "That is where she was shot," I blurted out. "At that window." We later read that a woman had been at her table, having coffee, when a stray bullet ended her life.

If we take the time to quiet our self talk and allow it, most of us can feel the history of a place. Gettysburg was my first slap in the face with it; the pain and desperation were almost enough to make me pass out at times. I had not yet learned to construct a distance between me and that world.

It is wonderful to feel the holiness emanating from a sacred well, a well-worn path through an ancient forest, the quiet of a cathedral. However, the earth also remembers so much sorrow and pain and feeling that is not always so wonderful.

I believe not in ghosts, per se, but that places can retain the strong emotions that occurred there. Like a tape recording or photo of a past event, the emotions continue to replay themselves and continue to be reinforced as we sense and experience them again.

For example, in Turkey I visited the house in which the Virgin Mary was said to have died. It was a quiet, unassuming shrine, but filled with hundreds of devout Christians and Muslims paying homage to the Mother. Outside was a well and an ancient olive tree where pilgrims tied bits of cloth with wishes and prayers. As each pilgrim worshiped and bathed their aura in the energy, a part of them also stayed and enhanced the emotion of the place.

I toured another famous battlefield almost thirty years after my first experience at Gettysburg. Culloden is a tragic part of Scottish history—the field where the British forces massacred brave Scots who fought for their freedom. With more life experience under my belt, I knew that I was likely to face a difficult time with the tour.

That morning I found a few minutes to walk barefoot on the grass in front of our rental house. I felt the strength of the earth, pulling it up through my feet and visualizing the energy moving up my body to my heart and mind. I asked that I be granted the knowledge that any pain I felt was from the past; that it was others' pain, not mine. I prayed for an open heart filled with compassion, but also the wisdom to know that what I felt and saw was in the past.

It made Culloden an achingly beautiful experience. As the crowds entered the site there was an immediate stillness; even the small children seemed to feel that this ground was sacred with the blood shed there.

Build up your Psychic Shields

As you travel, please take a few moments to build up your psychic shields before entering sites that may have witnessed great tragedy. Another quick protective gesture is to envision a bubble of light around you (your auric field) that repels any negative energy coming at you. I often envision myself inside a green balloon, with the painful energy just raindrops hitting my shield.

think it is bad or cowardly to avoid plac-

ill drain you emotionally. I, personally,

g Auschwitz. I feel a great connection

know that it would affect me greatly

a concentration camp. Our cousin's sister-in-

s held in a Japanese internment center near Borneo *during* the war. She went on to thrive after the war, getting her medical degree and living in Holland very successfully. In her fifties she went to a conference in Poland and went as a day trip to one of the concentration camps. It triggered a deep, unexpected reaction in her from which she never fully recovered. Her depression deepened and she ultimately took her own life.

As a mental health professional I would call it Post Traumatic Stress Disorder that had been triggered by exposure to such a similar situation to the one that she had experienced in Borneo. I can also put on my intuitive hat and say that the deep resonance of the pain of the past that was held in the camp directly triggered her spiritual, psychic reaction.

When we were planning to go to Vietnam Kathryn and I talked at length about some of the sites on our itinerary. We very purposefully chose NOT to go to the Chi Chi Tunnels where the Vietnamese lived underground and ambushed the American troops and were in turn trapped by Americans. It was hell for both armies, and atrocities were committed on both sides. Our husbands went and came back subdued and glad to have seen it. Kathryn and I had a massage at the hotel and felt glad to have missed it.

Take care of yourself when traveling and listen to your intuitive voice. Will it be too much for you to experience the killing fields of Cambodia? Does visiting your mother's *grave bring back memories and feelings you don't wish to relive? There is no shame in not going there. Honor yourself and your travel needs by listening to your inner voice.*

Raising your energy field

There is an electrical and magnetic field that surrounds every living being. This field is measurable and observable through many sophisticated tests such as an MRI or CAT scan, but is also easily seen with and felt by your third eye. Sometimes called Chi or Prana or halo, your human energy field or aura is distinctive to you and easily observable by using our third eyes. Being able to control the size of your aura provides you with a type of psychic protection because people seldom enter into another person's energy field unless invited. So, if you decide to shut down your third eye you should probably increase your energy field to compensate for it.

You raise your energy field in the same way you do most things … by intentionally deciding to do it. I always carry dowsing rods with me when I train police officers. I love to watch while a group of uniformed officers point dowsing rods at each other and roar with laughter. I have the officers break into pairs and ask them to stand fifteen feet or so away from each other. One officer holds a pair of dowsing rods (simple L shaped metal rods that can be purchased or made easily with wire coat hangers) in front of his body, far enough away from his body that the rods aren't swinging back to pick up his own field. He is then instructed to walk slowly toward the other officer. When the rods reach that person's energy field or aura, the rods will naturally swing out or together. How they swing is individual to the person and will vary from person to person and dowser to dowser.

Just seeing this phenomena is usually enough to make even the most hardened cop believe in the human energy field. The really useful part is when they realize that, even though they may not have previously even known they HAD an energy field, they have complete control of it. To demonstrate this, I first walk slowly toward a subject until the rods cross or move. This shows where the person's energy field begins, usually a foot or less from the body. I then ask him to consciously send out his energy field…to make it bigger. When I am asked how to do this, I respond that he just knows how to do it. Like everything in life, it is done with intent—you just do it.

Once the person has sent out his energy field, I walk slowly toward him again. In all likelihood, the rods will move or separate when I am much farther away from him then the first time I measured his field. He has, without knowing how, expanded his aura.

Of course, we can also pull our energy field in. We unconsciously hold our energy field in whenever we feel fearful, angry, sad, or threatened. To demonstrate this, I ask my subject to think of someone or something they are angry with, then repeat the exercise. When I do this demonstration, I often have to walk right up to the person, even touching them with the rods, before I hit their energy field.

So, what does this have to do with psychic wandering? Well, the larger your energy field is, the less likely you are to be interfered with or harassed. When I train police, I always tell them to send their energy field out in dangerous situations. Once they are aware of the impact their energy field has on others, they can send it out when they feel threatened or intimidated, rather than the natural reaction of pulling it in. By doing so they are much less likely to encourage confrontation. People just intuitively step out of others' auras unless invited.

Learning to control your energy field is like having a secret weapon against boundary intruders, tailgaters, and psychic vampires. When you consciously send out your aura, you are creating a bubble of protection around yourself. An interesting experiment is to send your energy field out when you are on a crowded elevator and watch the people around you move out of your field. I also create a field around my car whenever I am being tailgated and watch the other car back away from me.

Once, when I was traveling in China, I became separated from my companions while in the Forbidden City. People in China have a far different sense of physical boundaries than do Americans and have absolutely no difficulty pressing close to you, even to the point of knocking you over. On that day, the crowd was so immense and tight around me that I could feel a panic attack about to strike. Luckily, I remembered that I could send out my aura. I was pleased to discover that, even with their different sense of boundaries, the Chinese still did not wish to encroach on a stranger's energy field. In the midst of the crowd, a type of bubble formed around me, allowing me to walk swiftly away.

When you wish to shut your third eye down and get a little relief from extraneous psychic information that you don't want to know, you should increase your energy field as a type of auric protection. Also, whenever you feel threatened or frightened, try sending out your aura. It is a useful tool when walking in an unfamiliar part of town, or even just going to a job interview. A large energy field is unconsciously perceived by others as you being large and powerful.

Many years ago my husband and I were walking on the streets of Amsterdam and became lost. We always seem to get lost at least once per country. We found ourselves in the Red Light district and, even during the day, some of the streets seemed very threatening. Amsterdam is a city laced with canals over which there are hundreds of bridges. In order for us to return to our hotel, we had to cross a bridge in a rather frightening area. As we were crossing, a group of about six young men came toward us, walking abreast and completely blocking the bridge. While we couldn't tell their intent, it was clear that they were attempting, at least, to intimidate us. To get back to our hotel, however, we had no choice but to walk through them and cross the bridge.

Trying to stay out of judgment and fear, I sent my aura out as far as I could. Doing that immediately made me feel more confident and so I smiled at the group and walked toward them.

It felt a little as if waters were parting for us. The men separated enough to allow us to pass easily, then closed their ranks behind us. I will never know, of course, if sending my aura out had anything to do with the peaceful way we were allowed to pass. I do know it helped me to escape the fear that threatened to immobilize me. Since that time I have vowed to be very intentional with the size of my aura, particularly in situations that might seem threatening.

These techniques for controlling your third eye will be extremely valuable wherever you wander. Always remember to ask "Is it mine?" when hit with emotions or physical issues that come out of the blue. If it is not yours, it should go away with asking that question. Also remember to use your energy field as a type of protection and remember that the size of it is completely under your control. These two tools are far more valuable than any weapons or protection you can carry. Leave the pepper spray at home. Your auric field is far more effective, cheaper, and lighter to carry.

Create your own haven

Another marvelously effective tip for feeling safe on vacation is to create your own little nest or haven. Jean is a master of nest making. I think she was a bird in a past life. Here are some rituals that she uses to create a haven while traveling, although the techniques are just as effective in your own home.

I used to have terrible trouble sleeping on vacation. No matter how tired I was or how much I needed to sleep, the first night in a new bed meant no sleep. And if one is changing hotels every day or two the long sleepless nights tossing about become physically and mentally challenging.

I worked in a job where I had frequent work-related overnight trips, and this finally prompted me to ask myself why I was not sleeping. After meditating for over an hour I found my answer ... I did not feel safe. Every sound jolted me awake, the feel of a different pillow constantly reminded me that I was not in my own bed, and worry over missing a wake-up call had me awake before dawn.

Apparently, much as I love to travel, I am also a creature who needs her nest. I have eventually developed a two-prong approach to getting a good night's sleep.

First, the practical. I have determined what I absolutely need to feel at "home" in any hotel space or guest room. A travel alarm with fresh batteries tops my list. I immediately set it to the current time zone and on my night stand it goes. It also holds a small photo of my cats to remind me of them. My sense of smell is keen, and I absolutely must carry a bit of home with me (no, not litter box spray) so I always have a small travel candle in my toiletry bag. Next, I bring out my blow-up neck pillow from the plane. It can take the place of an uncomfortable hotel pillow, act as a back rest in a bad chair, even deflate and plug a hole in the screen of a window in Kenya. Lastly, I always carry my favorite tea bags (Twinings black currant, ginseng, and vanilla herbal). I have found that no matter how primitive the location, every kitchen has purified hot water for tea available.

Now, the spiritual. As I settle into my room, I place the candle and alarm clock, inflate my little pillow and put out two tea bags. I slowly circle the room and really notice all the lovely things about it, trying not to see the water spot on the ceiling, but rather focusing on the view or the delightful handmade basket that holds the soap. Then I light my candle and as the scent fills the air I ask for safe shelter and comfort from the space. I thank the room for giving me a bed to sleep in and the chance to rest. I remember how lucky I am to be here, experiencing a part of the world I have never seen before.

All of this really takes just a few minutes after I have arranged my shampoo in the bathroom and unpacked my nightgown. But it has made all the difference in the world. Often I feel that the physical space actually changes before my eyes into a more welcoming, sheltering place.

Our perceptions really build our realities. For me, I tend to see the negative and focus in with laser-sharp clarity on every flaw. A spot on the carpet quickly becomes a murder scene or a hair in the bathroom means the whole room should be condemned.

My husband and I stayed in a tent in the Costa Rica jungle, right on the shore of the Pacific Ocean. Our tent was large, had a wooden floor and an attached toilet and sink. There was no electricity, but the lantern light was lovely at night. Down a raised plank walk way was an open air building that served as dining hall and gathering place. It was the full-time job of one man to sweep out the scorpions and spiders as well as keep the monkeys off the table.

We were well warned on the protocols to follow. No food in the tents, check all your shoes before putting them on, zip up the netting over the bed when going to sleep to keep the critters out. Oh, and if the Howler Monkeys that live in the tree over your tent are agitated, be careful … they often throw feces down at tourists.

Our first night I retreated to the small toilet area to undress as the tents were quite transparent. I threw my T-shirt and shorts over the small dividing wall. Running to the bed, I landed on the rock hard surface and my husband, Fred, zipped us in for the night.

The minute our lantern was off my eyes adjusted and I could see an animal on the canvas roof. I grabbed my flashlight and spent most of the night with it pointed up to the blurred figure, I swear it would move incrementally the moment the flashlight was extinguished.

I must have fallen asleep from exhaustion at some point. Come morning I was telling Fred that we were NOT staying for five days in this tent but checking out immediately. "We could have been killed in the night by the animal." I explained. With great patience he balanced on the beds and looked over the plastic netting that enveloped them. There was my tee shirt that I had thrown over the bathroom divider the night before.

I am still not certain how that T-shirt managed to move all night! But we did finish out our stay, and saw marvelous things and had wondrous experiences. I never did fully embrace the dangers of tenting in the jungle or the bugs, but I would not trade the memories for anything. A sloth literally rolled on my feet, the birds welcomed us with delight at sunrise, even the Howlers seemed used to us by the time we left.

I hope that if I return now my little rituals would ease my fears and I would have noticed the sounds of the jungle instead of the small tear in the pillow case.

By focusing on the positive gifts that the room offers me, and by inviting relaxation and comfort in, I am able to create a bit of home and safety in my new environment. And by setting the intent that I am safe and the Universe is taking care of me I believe I do create safety.

Mark your territory

Many people create this same type of nest in their offices and even vehicles. When I worked as a probation officer, I always chuckled at how each person decorated their cubicle with what was important to them. Some had dozens of pictures of their children, others had tiny plastic toys to play with when stressed. My office had a small crystal and a potted plant. It became a way for us to label who we were and to personalize the drab government office building.

We also worked with a group of clients who were not particularly good at honoring other people's property and safety. So, I believe that our little cubicle decorations served the function of keeping us secure. Like many animals, we were, in our fashion, intuitively marking our territory. The message we were giving was that this little corner of the world was our domain and that we were in charge. The felons we worked with were being told, in a very subtle way, what they needed to honor in order to get along with their POs.

Whether you are traveling abroad, settling into a new workplace or decorating your home, it is always wise to leave a bit of yourself in your surroundings. Marking your territory with your intuitive signature is a great way to make sure only good intended people and things will feel comfortable entering.

Listen for intuitive messages

The final way to travel with protection is to make sure you listen when your intuition is giving you a message. This is important, of course, no matter where you are, whether at home or abroad. It can literally save your life. All the intuitive flashes and insights that we receive are worthless if we don't act upon them. I often tell my students that intuition without action is dead.

When you are traveling, in particular, it is a good practice to start each day with a simple question to your intuition. All you need to ask is: "Is there anything I need to know about today?" Sit quietly for a few minutes and just watch your thoughts, noting any emotions that might come to the surface or any physical sensations you might experience. All of these might give you a clue as to what you should watch for or be prepared for that day.

Your intuition will not always explain *why* you need to do something. It would be easier, I suppose, if your intuition sent you an email explaining everything it tells you. More likely, though, you will just hear a short message, see a mental picture, or feel an emotion or a physical sensation. I have learned that it is wise to trust these messages, even when they don't make any sense.

A few years ago Loren and I were traveling in Mexico, staying at a nice resort while soaking up sun and relaxing. One day we decided to take a break from the beach and head to downtown Mazatlan. When we travel, we always leave our valuables in the hotel safe, but I carry a bag with sunglasses, a small amount of money, a credit card, and a few other things I might need during the day. That day, though, as I picked up my bag to leave, I heard these words in my head: "Leave the bag here." I ignored it at first, knowing we would be gone a full day and wanting to have sunblock and tissues and all the other little things that make wandering easier. But, as I headed out the door, I heard it again. "Leave the bag here."

After years of practice, I am good at trusting intuitive messages, especially if I hear something twice. I have learned that when you don't trust your intuition you often get a good story. "My intuition told me not to drive down that road but I did anyway and got into an accident." When you DO trust your intuition the story isn't as good. "My intuition told me not to drive down that road, so I didn't...and nothing happened." I have learned from hard experience that it is better to have a good life than a good story. So, I left the bag in the hotel room, stuffing just a few pesos in a pocket.

We had a great time visiting the Mazatlan Cathedral, town square and market, then hiked up a small hill to get a few photos of the ocean and city. On the way back down we decided to take a scenic route down a quiet residential street, rather than take the busier main route. We were happily walking though a secluded, quiet area when three young Mexican men came running toward us.

My husband was carrying our small, very inexpensive point-and-shoot camera on a strap around his wrist. One of the men headed straight for Loren, grabbing the camera and snapping the strap off his wrist. As Loren tried to save it, the camera flew from them both and landed in the street. While I watched both Loren and the man dive for it, I realized that another young man was running straight for me.

He stopped a few feet before me, seemingly perplexed. I have to admit several choice words came out of my mouth that I had never before said to anyone. He stopped short, a look of disgust and disappointment on his face. I almost laughed when I realized he had just seen that I simply had nothing that he could steal or grab.

The whole mugging was over in a matter of moments. Amazingly, Loren had won the struggle over the camera and the three men had run away after realizing we had nothing worth stealing.

I am certain that if I had been carrying a bag it would have been grabbed away from me. While there may not have been anything of value in the bag, I most certainly could have been hurt in the struggle. My intuition had very likely saved me from harm. Luckily, Loren's struggle over the camera only resulted in a tiny cut on one hand and a dent in the camera.

Both Loren and I learned a bit about ourselves that day. He learned he fights back. I learned it was wise to listen to my intuition. I also learned I was capable of swearing at someone when needed.

Jean has similar stories of listening to and acting upon her intuition, except hers happened close to home.

Following my intuition and choosing a different path may have saved my life. I got in the car to return a rental DVD. I had always driven exactly the same route to the store for the past fifteen years. When I got in the car that day I turned left instead of right and took side streets. I honestly had no idea why, just that I felt an intuitive urge to avoid the busier and quicker route. On the evening news we heard that a car had been highjacked at the stop sign a block from our house, the woman raped and murdered within minutes of my departure from our house. I truly believe that opening myself to intuitive insights and giving myself permission to listen may have saved me.

My husband had a similar experience. He had a routine for his trip home from the office, leaving at the same time and traveling the same route. As he was leaving one afternoon he had the eerie feeling that he was missing something, and he had an urge to return to his desk. He listened to his intuition, returned to his cubicle, but could find nothing he had forgotten. Fifteen minutes later he was approaching the bridge over the Mississippi that he traveled daily when he saw a cloud of dust ahead. The 35W bridge had collapsed, killing thirteen people and injuring 145. If he had not delayed, he very well might have been one of those people.

These are dramatic stories of acting on one's intuition, stories where we know what the outcome might have been had we ignored our intuitive voice. But I believe that daily we are faced with many, many chances to either listen to or ignore our inner knowing. Often we will never know what might have happened if we had gone into the store we suddenly want to avoid as the outcome will not make the evening news. That does not mean that Spirit has not led us away from a dangerous or unhealthy choice.

chapter five

*What we see depends mainly
on what we look for.*

—JOHN LUBBOCK

Fairies and Spirits
and Orbs, Oh My!

I have always been fascinated by the realm of the elementals. Elementals are those creatures that exist both within our world and the spiritual realm. They are the spirits of air, fire, water, and earth, who live comfortably in all of these places. Elementals are called by many names (devas, nature spirits, gnomes, sometimes even angels) but my favorite name for them is fairies (or the alternative spelling, faeries).

The first time I saw a fairy I was a very small girl. My grandfather used to take me down to the river where we would sit quietly, watching for fairies and other magical creatures. We were a peculiar pair, Grandpa and me. I was a sickly child, unable to run and play with the other children, and he was known as the town "eccentric," a man with a booming voice and a gentle manner who never could hold a job or fit in with what passed for society in the small Minnesota town of Hinckley. Nobody could ever really tell me what was wrong with Grandpa, only that he had returned from World War I by way of what they called a sanatorium. Since then he had plenty of time to sit quietly and watch fairies.

We would walk to the Grindstone River, across the dirt road from my grandparent's tiny farm. After we reached the riverbed, we turned to the right and went up a small bluff to a hidden knoll. It was filled with ferns and lichen-covered rocks. Grandpa taught me to search for the johnny-jump-ups, lilies of the valley, and jack-in-the-pulpits that were hidden amid the fallen logs and ancient stones.

It was truly a mystical place and one where it seemed only right to talk in whispers. It was our secret spot, where our club of two would hold weekly meetings. Sitting was one of Grandpa's best skills, or at least that's what Grandma always said. He taught me to sit for hours, looking at the glade with "gentle eyes." I learned to unfocus my sharp young vision until the green of the ferns melted and flowed into the shimmering of the air. Then, when the only sound was my own breath, I saw my first fairy.

Fairies are shy creatures. Grandpa said they were curious and couldn't help but come to see why such huge creatures were in their world. "But," he said, "you never look directly at a fairy. They are very private and hide their mysteries beneath their wings."

The fairies were our special secret, Grandpa said. Seeing them was a reward for being still. "Only very unique people like us," he said, "would have the patience or the time to catch a glimpse of their veiled world." I agreed. Even at five years of age, I was fairly certain no one would believe that I had actually seen fairies. Of course, I already knew that no one listened to Grandpa at all.

Fifty-some years later, I still believe in fairies but, like most adults, I have not taken the time or had the intention to seek them out for a very long time.

Just recently though, I took a group of spiritual seekers on a Celtic mystery tour of Ireland. Before we went, I decided that this was the trip when I would seek out and talk again to the fairies.

The first few days were hectic. We viewed the Book of Kells, marveled at the wonder of Newgrange, sampled fine food and a few pints of Guinness and toured the green land of the Irish. On the fourth day of the trip I was rather tired and opted out of a long hike to see some ruins in the pouring rain. Dee, one of the group members, stayed behind with me and, when the sun suddenly appeared, we decided to take a leisurely stroll down the paths of Glendalough. Glendalough is the site of a thousand-year-old monastery surrounded by even more ancient woods and meadows.

The sun on the rain-soaked greenery and trees was incredibly lovely. Dee and I walked in silence and wonder through the magical scenery and I said a quiet hello to the elementals. Then, peeking out from behind a tree, was a fairy. Both Dee and I stopped, watching the small colored lights that twinkled around the fairy and marveling at the wonder of it all. I quietly asked for permission to take its picture. Aiming my camera in the direction I had last seen movement, I snapped several frames, then moved down the path, stopping every once and again to take a few more photos.

The air was fresh from the fallen rain and the forest sparkled with life. I had no doubt that we had entered into a fairy realm. "Still," I wondered, "had I been able to capture anything with my camera?" After all, fairies are shy and have seldom been captured on film. When I looked at my photos that evening I was thrilled to discover that I had a picture of what I truly believe is a fairy. A photo taken seconds before shows nothing, as does the photo taken a short time after. There was nothing near the site that could possibly reflect to create the image.

A fairy dancing in the grove.

While I suspect there will be much skepticism and explanations about the photo, I realize I don't really care. I don't need a photograph to prove to me the existence of fairies. I have known that since I was four years old. What the experience did for me was to remind me of how very little we see sometimes, if we don't take the time to look.

You certainly do not need to travel in Ireland to see a fairy. In fact, I have caught glimpses of them in my front yard. What traveling does, though, is give you permission, if you are willing to take it, to slow down, ask, and wait to see the elemental realm.

I very much doubt that I would have seen anything magical if I had not stayed behind from the larger group. All the travelers were interested in the mystical, but fifteen people walking on a path is far too noisy and overwhelming for the fairy realm. I thought I was staying behind just to stay dry, but I now believe I was set up in this way so that the fairies could say hello to me.

How to see elementals and fairies

If you are interested in seeing the elemental realm, you must first learn to be still and quiet. There are certain types of habitat that fairies prefer, although they can be seen almost everywhere. Their favorite place, though, is in a glen or forest. They love ferns and moss and wild flowers. They are far happier in a wild environment than a structured garden. Look for them in "sparkling" places, where rocks take on a shine and water dances. They love streams, ponds, and rivers.

Fairies are most often found in what is called "tween" places. Tween places are those areas where two things meet, making it difficult to tell, sometimes, which is one and which is the other. Examples are places like shorelines, where water and land meet in a constantly shifting fashion, or the horizon, where earth and sky sometimes seem to blend. Other tween places are between the grass and the dirt or a leaf and a branch. Fairies linger in places that are not quite one thing or another. They love the slippery uncertainty of change. They slip between dimensions of time and place in a way that is dizzying to us humans.

Fairies also love the tween times. Tween times are times of the day or season when things are about to shift. When it is hot one day and cold the next. When the rain has ceased falling but it is not quite dry. When it is not yet winter but autumn is over. These are times when we are closest to the veil between Spirit and earth. It is also that time of day when soft light lingers even after the sun has slipped below the horizon or when you can see a hint of light just before dawn. Dawn and dusk are tween times, as are solstices, eclipses, and equinoxes. It is no wonder that their favorite festivals are Beltane (May 1) and Samhain (what we call Halloween). Faeries and other mystical folk love the tween times because they can so easily slip back and forth between the realms.

It is always wise to use soft eyes when looking for elementals. Sharply focused eyes are wonderful for all our analytical endeavors, but, for viewing the magical realm it is always best to keep your eyes slightly unfocused. Fairies tend to be seen from the corner of your eyes. They are the little bright lights or flashes of color that you see sometimes when you are not quite looking at anything and therefore seeing everything.

Of course, like all folk, fairies and elementals like politeness. They consider it rude to demand to see them. They hate being photographed without their consent. You will be surprised and thrilled to see how cooperative they will be, though, if you ask politely and then wait until they are ready. Seeing elementals must always be on their schedule and their terms. After all, you are the visitor in their world.

Elementals and fairies can be tricksters. The day after I took my fairy picture I loaded it onto my iPad to show to the members of my group. Then, all week, I worried that the photo would somehow just disappear. Fairies are like that. They give as they see fit and steal back when they feel like it.

On your journeys, whether to a local park around the corner or an exotic country across the world, give yourself the gift of a day or at least a few hours to look for fairies. Find someplace quiet, sit softly, and unfocus your eyes. Then just gaze, especially at tween places…and wait. The odds are rather high that you will see something, perhaps sparkles or unknown movement or even a ripple in the air. Try not to worry too much about defining what you are seeing. That can come later, if you must do so. I think you will find that, whether you see elementals or not, you will be richly rewarded by the attempt.

Orbs

While photographing a fairy is a rare event, photographing orbs has become very commonplace. I get so many orbs in my photos sometimes that they have become almost annoying. No one really knows what they are or why they are appearing in photos with increasing frequency. All we know is that the advent of digital photos has made orbs something that almost everyone photographs on occasion.

I have read that the explanation for orbs in photographs is dust in the air, reflections, water on a camera lens, or any number of other stories. In my opinion, none of those explanations really make sense. You can take ten pictures of the same exact site, all within minutes of each other, and get orbs on one picture and not on any of the others. One photo can have one orb, the very next have none, and the last one have a dozen. If orbs were solely caused by water on the lens or dust, then all the pictures taken within minutes of each other should have that imperfection.

Often these orbs seem to contain faces or figures within them. Usually they are round, but occasionally they are other shapes. I have had three or four people snap a picture at exactly the same time and at the same object, and only had orbs appear on one camera. The truth is, no one truly knows why they appear but many people have ideas.

The most impressive orbs I have photographed were around the tomb of Archbishop Oscar Arnulfo Romero in a cathedral in San Salvador. I have found that nearly all centers of worship, from Catholic cathedrals to Buddhist temples or Hindu Ashrams, have a holy feel and many spirits also come to worship there. When I travel, my favorite places to visit are holy places so I have spent a great deal of time in temples and churches and cemeteries and ruins. Nowhere, though, have I found more powerful orb energy than at Father Romero's tomb.

Archbishop Oscar Arnulfo Romero was an outspoken champion for peace, human rights, and dignity for the El Salvadoran people. During a time of growing unrest in the country of El Salvador, he informed the world about all the people who had been tortured, slaughtered, and just disappeared in his country. He was nominated for a Nobel Peace Prize in 1979 and, in March of 1980, he was assassinated before the altar of a small chapel as he was saying Mass. It is believed that his assassins were members of the Salvadoran death squad.

Ever since his assassination, his tomb in a corner of the Metropolitan Cathedral in San Salvador is continually bedecked with flowers left by Salvadorans and visitors from other countries. People pray there, and it has become a shrine where it is reported many healing miracles have occurred. The tomb shimmers with a light all its own. All of my photographs of his tomb were filled with sparkling orbs, one of which contains the head of a man.

Orbs at Archbishop Romero's tomb.

How to capture orbs on film

So, what are orbs? I believe they are energy signatures and that today's more sophisticated cameras are increasingly picking up these signatures. Some orbs, like the one at Romero's tomb, will contain a figure of some type. Most are circular but some have other shapes. The majority are white, but some contain colors. They are, if nothing else, a reminder to us that we are at a site that is full of spirits, energy, and usually holiness.

Almost all the orbs I have captured by camera have been at ruins, tombs, or churches. Sometimes though, they appear around people. When this happens, I believe the energy is there because, for many different reasons, the occasion is holy.

I use the word holy differently than most people might. Holy to me does not mean religious, although many religious sites are holy. Holy is a state of being in which the person strives to be and see more than is apparent with his or her physical eyes. Holy is seeing with the soul and the heart. Skyscrapers can be holy if the energy is right. I am told that ground zero at the World Trade Center is a prime place for capturing orbs of all types.

The best way to capture orbs is to go to a place that feels holy to you. It doesn't have to be a church or cemetery, it could be your backyard or even your living room. I had one friend who captured spectacular orbs around dusk, just off her deck. Once you have decided on your place, start snapping photos. It is usually good to aim at an object, such as a tombstone or tree or building. That way you have something the orb can contrast against. Try to avoid aiming at shiny surfaces as you might capture a reflection that will make it uncertain if there was also an orb there.

Luckily, with digital photographs, you can take photos to your heart's content without spending anything more than time. One of the fascinating things about orbs is that you might take fifty photos in a matter of moments and the orbs will only show up in one or two. To me that demonstrates that the orb is a real phenomenon, not merely a reflection or water drop. If that were true, it should show up in two photos taken within seconds of each other. Lastly, don't worry too much about what you captured. Just enjoy the experience and rejoice in the results.

Ghosts

It may seem a little strange coming from someone like me, but I don't really believe in ghosts, at least in the way most people think of them. I do, however, not only believe in but see spirits often. I use the term spirits rather than ghosts to describe souls of people who have died and passed on to what I call the realm of Spirit. Some people refer to that realm as heaven or by many other names. Whatever you call it, the soul has left the body and yet continues to have a vibrant and joyful life in another realm. It can, though, make appearances here on Earth, at least in a fashion. Spirits often try to communicate with us … and they do. They also are able to return to earth plane in an etheric body and come here for a variety of reasons. It is similar to how we have many reasons to travel. In my experience, though, they do not stay here on the earth, stuck and haunting us.

In the many years I have been doing this type of work and having talked to hundreds of spirits, I have yet to meet what others describe as a ghost. (Meaning a spirit who is trapped, haunting a place on earth.) What I have seen, often, are places in which there is an energy loop that contains some of the features and memories of someone who has passed. This is,

I believe, what most people are seeing when they see what they call a ghost.

The best way I can describe this phenomenon is that it is similar to a morphic field. The term morphic field was coined by Rupert Sheldrake who, in studying plant mutations, learned that cell patterns have a type of memory, not explainable only by genetics. This memory, which Sheldrake called morphic resonance, increases the likelihood that mutations will recur. The memory extends beyond the cells and into magnetic fields far beyond the surface of the earth.

Strong emotions, such as those that happen in violent deaths, also create a type of morphic field. It is an energy loop that replays over and over again in the same location. In a so-called haunted location, I often see these energy or memory loops. The emotions, often of fear, anger, and sadness, are very real. Sometimes there is even a type of wispy image that can be seen, or a sort of cold emptiness. Sometimes, if you are lucky, you might even be able to catch this image on your camera or even pick up sounds on a recording. Because it is an energy loop, the ghost appears to do the same thing over and over, or repeat the same phrase again and again. If you ever see a spirit that is constantly repetitive, that allegedly can't move on, it is likely an energy loop, caused by a morphic emotional field. Real spirits, on the other hand, are constantly growing, changing, and moving—just like we do. They are never trapped in the human realm. If they are here it is because they have come for a purpose, generally to say hello to a loved one or to watch over someone.

It is fun, though, to use our third eye to see and read these energy loops. Like all things mystical, seeing this energy field is often simply a matter of intending to see it. There are many, many of these fields playing in places like cemeteries, hospitals, and hotels. If you wish to experience that type of thing, you need to use an open mind and unfocused eyes—just as we have discussed about seeing so many phenomena.

New Orleans, especially prior to Hurricane Katrina, was a place where morphic energy loops were in abundance. Jean and I visited in the late 1990s and had a wonderful time experiencing the magic of that city. Ever since she was a child, Jean has had a fascination with cemeteries. On our visit to New Orleans the raised tombs of the many cemeteries called to her to visit.

The aboveground tombs in the cemeteries of New Orleans are often referred to as cities of the dead. As Jean and I entered the gates of one such city we were greeted by decorative, rusty ironwork and sun-bleached marble tombs. Crosses and statues on tomb tops cast contrasting shadows that added to the sense of mystery. The living relatives of the dead often leave burning votive candles, photographs, and small gifts of food or drink for their loved ones in Spirit. All of this contributes to the feeling that you have entered a holy and mystical place.

We walked through the cemetery marveling at its mystery and beauty when Jean stopped, suddenly, in front of a large crypt. "Take my picture," she ordered me, handing me her camera. "Now."

I was surprised. First, she never lets me take pictures. Also, the place that she wanted me to photograph was not even very attractive. It was a ruin of a crypt with no fancy iron work, statues, or scroll work. Still, I obediently snapped a photo.

When we got home, she developed the roll of film and discovered that, in addition to her being on the photo, we had captured several other filmy figures, dancing all around her. After seeing the photo I realized why she had been so insistent about having her picture taken at that exact spot. While her conscious mind could not have explained it at the time, her intuitive mind must have told her that there were spirits lurking who wanted their photograph taken. Unfortunately, those photos have been lost and can't be included in this book.

Sometimes spirits are so insistent about having their picture taken that they actually barge right into a photo opportunity. A number of years ago we were part of a rather large group of friends and family who toured Turkey together. One of the things Jean and I had always wanted to do was to have tea at the Pera Palace Hotel in Istanbul, the fabled end point of the Orient express as told by Agatha Christie. The hotel is elegant and reeks of history and intrigue. Our group of eight enjoyed drinks and coffee and soaking in the ambiance, then decided to memorialize our outing with a group picture taken on a lovely sloping staircase.

We posed as a group on the staircase, asking a waiter to take our picture. Because several people had cameras, the waiter had to oblige us with numerous shots. When Jean had hers developed though (this was before digital photography was common), Jean's camera's shot showed an extra person in the photo. The man on the top right-hand side is my husband, Loren. The man next to him is a stranger who did not appear on any of the other photos taken at virtually the same time. Furthermore, no one could recognize him, and Loren swears he was on the top stair all by himself.

It is a little hard to believe that a total stranger would impose himself into our group photo and even harder to believe that none of us would have noticed him doing so.

I believe he was a morphic loop. Rather like a still movie that continues to play in the background, our cameras had captured him, even though no one's eyes had seen him.

The man at the upper left is the ghost. My husband (on the right) swears he was by himself. No one else noticed the man until the photo was developed.

Sometimes spirits may not be seen but will make their presence known in other ways. Here is a story from Jean telling how a spirit turned on a radio. Spirits are well known for using electronics to communicate with us, often changing channels or turning up the volume.

For almost twenty years we were best friends with a lovely couple, John and Colleen. They happily put up with our idiosyncrasies while we ignored their disbelief in anything magical. We often traveled with each other, and I think brought out the best in each other as we laughed and joked. One constant source of friction between John and me, however, was his need to ALWAYS have a radio on either in the car or the house we might be sharing. I hate noise, especially when it is a Mexican talk radio show in the Yucatan!

John was diagnosed with esophageal cancer at the age of forty-six and died three months later. There really was no time for the goodbyes we had hoped for as he worked toward a healing until the very last.

The fall after he died we asked his widow, Colleen, to come with us to the Netherlands for a very relaxed trip around the country, hoping it would be a break from her unremitting grief and the busyness of trying to rebuild her life and business without John.

We had a lovely time, and put over 1,500 miles on our rental car. It was one of our last days in Holland, Colleen was in the front seat and I was driving. From the back seat my husband Fred said, "Don't you wish John were here with us? I can almost feel him sitting here by me." Colleen laughed. John was over six feet tall and never sat in the back seat if at all possible. "No, he would have kicked me out of the front seat by now," she said.

Just then the radio came on, full volume, playing an oldie from the 1970s. I almost ran off the road. The car had an old-fashioned radio that required one to turn the knob on and off. There was no way we could have bumped it just then to have it come on.

Did I mention that John was the proud owner of a radio station that played "music from the best times of your life"? There is no doubt in any of our minds that John was travel-ing with us on that little road in Holland.

Whether you want to see ghosts or fairies or orbs, or any other mystical being, you do, of course, need to intend to do so. A good analogy for this is, surprisingly enough, bird watching.

A few years ago we were blessed to spend a couple of weeks in Costa Rica. Even more lucky was the fact that our guide turned out to be an experienced birder who carried mar-velous binoculars and other tools of the trade with him and taught us how to look for, identify, and see the birds. Up until that trip I knew birds existed, of course, but I had never real-ly paid any attention to them. So I didn't see many and didn't appreciate them when I did see them.

Our two-week sojourn in Costa Rica was both interest-ing and wet. Going to a rain forest, I learned, meant that it rained…a lot. The jungle was lush, moist, thick, and teem-ing with life. Yet only with a guide could I know where to point my binoculars. With his help, we entered a world of color and mystery and only a couple of things (like a very large tarantula) that terrified.

On a beach in Manuel Antonio, I chatted briefly with another traveler on a different tour. "How are you enjoying the country?" I asked. "It is lovely," she said, "but I am disappointed that we have seen so few birds and animals." I was uncharacteristically quiet. We had, at that point, counted nearly one hundred species of birds and mammals, along with countless butterflies and the occasional scary creepy thing. We saw far more birds because we had a brilliant guide, who seemed to recognize the call of every bird and see a flash of color when I could only see the verdant greenery.

We would be walking along a muddy path when he would suddenly stop for no apparent reason. Holding up his hand, we were signaled to halt quietly and wait. After a time he would point to a spot no one would have noticed. Then we could all see it. A resplendent quetzal … a pair of Macaws … a lazy sloth.

Shortly after I returned from this adventure, I was doing a reading. My client asked how I could see and hear things that others could not and the vision of my guide in the jungle appeared in my mind.

What I realized is that the spirit realm is exactly like the Costa Rican jungle. The spirits are not hiding … they are going about their lives. Yet, without stopping, being quiet, intentionally desiring to see and knowing what you are looking for, you will not see them any more than you will accidentally trip over a quetzal.

When one begins their journey into the world of spirits and elementals it is useful to have a guide. Later, we start to recognize the signs … just as I began after a few days to know where and how to spot birds. Then I learned to walk silently. I learned to use soft eyes and scan the tree tops for a hint of movement. The guide said, "Always look for movement, not color."

Good advice for looking for spirits and elementals. Walk gently and quietly. Scan for movement. Listen and look with soft gentle eyes and ears.

We live in a world teeming with life and spirits and magic, but we seldom take time to watch and listen and see. When was the last time you sat in silence and waited for movement? I encourage you all to take some time to go on your own adventure. It is an amazing and exciting world.

Other Elementals

Sometimes it is easy to believe that all the world thinks the same way we do. The beauty of traveling is that it dispels that myth very quickly. Most of the world's people are far more open to the reality of other beings. Small elemental creatures might be called faeries or Apus or gnomes or Tomten or one of a thousand other names for the wee ones. Here Jean tells of how traveling helped her remember about the little people.

As a little girl my maternal grandparents were often primary caregivers (our father's parents had died many years before my birth). They had grown up with Swedish as their first language even though they were third generation Americans. Our community was largely Swedish, and Minnesota is pretty darned Scandinavian still!

My dear Nana was what I would call a kitchen mystic, Christian to the core, but with a deep belief in what we would now call the paranormal. My Bampa was a rather unrepentant pagan who attended church every Sunday and prayer service on Wednesday night. Between the two of them we soon learned that dropping a fork meant some male company was coming soon ... better tidy up the kitchen; and that milk and bread must be left out for the barn elves every night or those Tomten would cause the chickens to stop laying.

I honestly had not thought a bit about my Scandinavian heritage when we decided to take a trip to Iceland. It was the cheapest vacation we could find, so off we went!

Iceland is a country with only three hundred thousand people, gorgeous in a dramatic and austere fashion. It is unspoiled and unpolluted, with the cleanest air imaginable. It is so close to the arctic circle that when we were there in June the sun never completely set, and we experienced an eerie sort of twilight at midnight. The population is one of the most highly educated and sophisticated in the world. Fifty-three percent of them believe in nature spirits.

I had returned to the belief system of my youth, and it was a life-changing experience. We stayed in a B&B in Reykjavik that was ultramodern and run by a married couple with degrees in computer programming. Our first morning there Hulla could not find her house keys and was looking everywhere. She said in all earnestness, "Where could the house elf have hidden them?" She then sheepishly looked at me and laughed. I told her of our Tomtens growing up, both in the barn and the house, and we exchanged elf stories for an hour before she took the bus in for shopping. The keys later turned up, she told us, under the floor mat.

Saevars was the driver we had hired for a few days of sightseeing outside of Reykjavik. I asked him about the recent controversy about building a road where some Trolls lived. Apparently a large boulder in the path of the road was home to some of the hidden folk (Huldufolk). In order to complete the road the boulder had to be moved but equipment repeatedly broke down as it approached the boulder, *and there were increasing accidents on the site. Finally a Troll communicator was brought in to explain the situation to the Huldufolk. The Trolls requested more time to move, which was granted by the government. Then, when they had moved, the communicator informed the road crew that work could commence. There were no further incidents in finishing the road, and the boulder was moved intact to another location.*

Saevars also told us that recently the first shopping mall had been built in Iceland. The European developers picked a site that was known to be close to several gnome dwellings, so all underground utilities and electrical cables were carefully rerouted to avoid any disturbance to them. He told these stories with a smile but, again, when I said that I believed in earth spirits he opened up and stated, "Those who do not believe in spirits must spend a midsummer night out in the hills."

It was amazingly affirming and freeing to be among intelligent, functional adults who could feel the pull of the earth beings. It brought my childhood back to life, while making me realize that the belief system espoused by modern-day America is not the universal. Feeling our earth as a living entity does not make one crazy; in fact it may be a sign of deep sanity.

Without the affirmation of this trip back to a home I never knew I had, I do not think I would have had the courage to learn to listen to Earth.

chapter six

When all's said and done, all roads lead
to the same end. So it's not so much which
road you take, as how you take it.

—CHARLES DE LINT

All Paths Lead
to the Same God

One of the great joys of traveling, at least for me, is learning
and experiencing the various ways in which people worship
and celebrate their connection to the Divine. I believe that
to fully understand a culture, you must experience the spiritual underpinnings of that land. The ways that our species
finds to worship are varied and unique. In the end, though, I
have learned that no matter how unusual and perhaps even
bizarre some practices are, compared to what I am used to,
all spiritual practices and paths are celebrating the same God.

One of the wonderful things about our modern culture is that you don't have to travel far to learn about different forms of religion, spirituality, and ritual. Just a few miles from my home we have a large Hindu temple, a Muslim mosque, a Buddhist temple and any number of Christian churches and Jewish synagogues. I have to admit, though, that I have visited very few of them. I think because it seems so much more exotic, I tend to leave my exploration of different forms of worship for my travels.

Many times, having to work or struggle to experience holiness seems to make it more valuable. I suppose it is human nature to think that we should have to work hard for things… even spiritual experiences.

A few years ago when I was in India I was drawn to go to a Hindu temple at Ranthambore. It is a small temple, dedicated to the Lord Ganesh, but it is a very popular place because the locals believe that Ganesh is able to bless devotees with prosperity. It is also on the top of a very high fortress on a tall hill. To get there we had to climb over six hundred steps and go through seven gates. We fell into the midst of a pilgrimage of sorts, with the people in lovely colorful dress and often adorned with painted faces. Every so often they would stop to sing and dance, beaming smiles at the foreigners who stuck out like sore thumbs in our running shoes, travel vests, and sun hats.

Dodging the pilgrims and the hundreds of monkeys that live in the fort, we finally made it to the small temple where we were invited in and allowed to ring a bell to get Ganesh's attention. After leaving a small offering, we were then blessed by a priest who tied several pieces of colorful string around my wrist. I was told that if I wore the string until it fell or rotted off of its own accord, my wish would be granted.

Although this temple is not a famous one, that experience was one of the most meaningful of that trip for me. I felt truly blessed and wore my strings until they were dirty and shabby looking. They never, though, showed any sign of falling off. Finally, weeks after returning home and having far too many people ask why I was wearing dirty strings around my wrist, I cut them off. I felt vaguely guilty doing so, not because I would not get my wish but because it felt irreverent to do so.

What was it that made me climb hundreds of steps in a blinding sun, walk on filthy floors in bare feet, and pay large fees to experience a tiny bit of holiness? I am rather certain that I would not have driven even a few miles to go to such an unassuming temple if it were near my house. I also know I would not have kept a dirty string around my wrist for weeks if someone I knew had placed it there. No, it was the allure of the unknown and unexplained and unusual that made it spiritual for me. Traveling often teaches us how to see the sacred in the profane. That is one of the reasons I travel.

When places are unique we have a tendency to be willing to do things that we would not otherwise do. One of my favorite places to travel is the Sacred Valley of Peru. Home of Machu Picchu, the sacred valley is brimming with many ancient and amazing Incan ruins. The views are breathtaking, the air fresh, the food incredible, and the people are kind and friendly. What sets the sacred valley apart from almost anywhere else in the world, though, is that spirituality and mysticism are a way of life, not just a way of thinking. It seems as if magic and ritual and joy are waiting for you around every corner.

My trip there in May 2011 was my third visit to Peru and I was a bit concerned that time might have modernized the sacred valley and dimmed its magic. I should not have worried. Peru, the sacred valley and Machu Picchu, as well as many other sacred sites, remained as full of mystery and magic as they always had.

Shamans in Peru live in the high Andes and are said to come down to the valley when they psychically know they are needed. On this trip, a Quero (an elder healer) and his daughter and helper arrived on the second day of our journey and traveled with us for several days. We were privileged and blessed to be able to participate in a Despacho ceremony with them. In a Despacho ceremony, the Shaman first arranges flowers, candy, coca leaves, grains, beer, and many other things, on white paper. These offerings are made to the Apus (mountain deities) and Pachamama (mother earth) and, after being painstakingly and lovingly created, the Despacho bundle is burned. Participants are invited to set their own intentions for the ceremony and to be part of the process. Doing this ceremony so early on in our trip allowed us to release things that might have held us back from fully embracing the lessons and joys of the journey.

A Despacho ceremony.

As luck would have it, we were in Peru that year for the festivals honoring the Chakana. The Chakana is the Andean Cross, which is inspired by the star constellation of the Southern Cross. At midnight on May 2 the Southern Cross reaches its highest position. So, there were parades and fiestas and just plain fun all over the town of Agua Callientes, which sits at the base of Machu Picchu. Since my birthday was May 4, I, being me, declared all the parades to be in honor of my birthday.

We were each given a necklace of the Chakana, which promotes safety, blessing, assistance, and fertility. Almost every house in the sacred valley has a cross, along with two pottery bulls and some grains, placed on the roofs of their houses, pointed toward the top of the mountains where the Apus reside and which is believed to increase the occupant's magical power.

This is the way of traveling in the sacred valley. Magic is almost expected, festivals break out spontaneously, you turn a corner and end up in a shrine or at an altar. All of this happens while you stand in a place so breathtakingly beautiful that the scenery screams for your attention at every stop.

If you can, participating in a holy ceremony while traveling can be life changing. Just as I would not necessarily go to a Hindu temple in my home town, I also know that a Despacho ceremony done in the sacred valley means more to me than if the same ceremony were done on my lawn. Why? Because when I travel I am braver. I am willing to set aside my judgments and doubts and embrace mystery. The rewards for doing this are so great that, even when I return home, some of that courage remains.

Despacho Ceremony Exercise

While there is something magical about doing a Despacho ceremony in Peru or a Feng Shui blessing ceremony in China, these ceremonies are just as powerful when done in your own home or yard. It is not the Shaman that creates the power. It is the participant's intention and respect for the mystery. Making a Despacho is an act of love, for yourself and for the earth. It is a reminder of the connections we share with the Divine, all beings, spirits, and sacred places. At the deepest level, it is an opportunity to enter into the essential unity of all things. You can create your own ceremony, either alone or with friends. The most important elements are a sense of joy and sacredness and the intention to honor the earth and let go of things that may be hampering your growth and joy.

Begin by laying on the ground a square of paper, or a cloth that you don't mind burning. Then, slowly and reverently lay things on your cloth that represent for you important items that nurture you. In Peru those things are usually grains, sugar, alcohol, and the ever-important coca leaves. In the United States, coca leaves are illegal. Instead, you might wish to use spice leaves such as bay or basil or even tobacco. You should add ingredients that you use in your own diet, including small candy bars, fruit, potato chips, or any other treats you enjoy. You can sprinkle these items with alcohol as they do in Peru or you can use diet coke or coffee or whatever your favorite beverage may be. Just do it with the intention of thanking the Universe for nurturing you.

You can then add representations of things you wish to bring into your life. The Peruvians often add small toy cars, play money, and other things. If you want to manifest a trip, draw a picture of airline tickets or a passport or add a photo of the place you want to visit. If you need a new house, draw out plans of what you want or cut a picture of your ideal home out of a magazine. If you want your relationship to improve or to find a new one, you can write out elements of what you need from a partner.

Finally, you can add representations of things you are willing to release from your life. Perhaps you wish to lay your cigarettes down or a copy of your overbooked schedule for the week. You can also just write a note stating what no longer serves you, blessing it, and letting it go. Spend some time arranging all these items to make your Despacho beautiful as well as functional, then fold it into a package and bind it with twine or ribbon.

The Peruvians touch the package to their crown and heart, blessing the package and saying a prayer of thanks. It is later burned, with the intentions and thanks going up to the Apus. You can do the same, sending your intentions to Heaven or wherever you believe they will be heard. This ceremony is as powerful as you make it. It focuses your attention on gratitude, intention, and release.

One of my challenges in life is some difficulty with my vision due to a botched eye surgery many years ago. So, when I get a chance to offer a prayer or make a wish or set an intention, I often wish/pray/hope for better vision. So far, my physical vision is about the same but I have had some vivid lessons and experiences based on my wish.

The first time this happened was at a conference only a few hours drive from my home. I was one of the keynote speakers at an international metaphysical and spiritual conference. Although I speak worldwide, and conduct intuition training for many diverse groups, it is rare for me to feel so at home at a conference as I felt at this symposium. My talk had been accepted with love and I felt surrounded by like-minded individuals. The entire week had been more of a vacation than a job for me and I was sorry to see it come to an end.

I had been told about the healing service that was considered by many to be the highlight of the week. It was held on the last night of the symposium. I had been invited to join the forty or so healers who took their place on the stage, but I had respectfully declined. I was a speaker, teacher, and palmist, but I did not consider myself a healer. Besides, I wished to watch from an observer's point of view and, perhaps experience some healing for myself.

I sat in one of the front rows, transfixed by the spectacle unfolding in front of me. The healers came from dozens of countries and incorporated as many healing traditions. Shamanistic healing was done next to those healing from a Christian tradition. Some healers prayed, some used touch, others moved in a dance fashion. Beauty, power, and love hung in the air. Earlier, I had decided to ask the Universe for improvement of my vision. I was one of the first of nearly four hundred to go onto the stage to experience the healing. I was directed to the chair in front of a minister with whom I had become acquainted earlier in the week. I knew that we both came from the Christian tradition and felt comfortable opening myself to her ministrations.

I could sense her hands stroking my aura, even though there was no actual physical touch. I silently prayed for clear sight as the power in her hands magnified. I felt a warm white light enter me through my crown, engulfing my body down to my toes. I had a sense that the Holy Spirit had touched me—then it was gone. I stood shakily and headed across the stage to my seat. As I stood momentarily at the stairs leading down off the stage, I gazed out at the audience. I was transfixed by the sight. All of the hundreds of people in the auditorium were glowing with a white light and were connected by thin golden strands. The sight was so beautiful that I was moved to tears.

As the service continued the audience filed past me on their way to the stage. As each person walked past me, I stared in awe. Never had I seen such beauty or felt such love. At that moment I was connected to everyone in the room. I knew everything about each person, all their fears, challenges, and dreams—and all I saw was beauty. Even after the service, the glow continued. There was a reception at which we chatted and drank coffee. At one point a woman approached me to ask for clarification about a palm reading I had given her earlier. As I again looked at her hand, the sensation of knowingness continued. Her life was opened to me in a way I had never before experienced—and it was exquisite!

The next day, the glow was gone and my intuitive knowing was back to its normal level. I had been changed in a way that I still cannot fully explain. My physical eyes had not been healed. Instead I had been given an opportunity to see with completely new vision. My prayer for clear sight had been granted in a way that I still cannot fully comprehend.

What I learned from that experience is that you have to be careful what you ask for. I had asked for clear vision and had been given it in a way I could not have predicted. I received a similar lesson on my trip to India. We were at a Hindu temple that was much larger and more elaborate than the one I described earlier. There was a large crowd there but I had somehow been pushed to the front, standing in front of three priests who were blessing the crowd. Again, I asked for better vision. Seconds later one priest, who had been splashing holy water over the crowd, tossed a large container of Ganges water in my direction. I blinked too slowly and my face and eyes were baptized with a huge splash of water.

I became immediately frightened and worried. We had just returned to Delhi from visiting the city of Varanasi, where we had taken a boat down the Ganges. The Ganges, I knew, was the most polluted river on earth. Pilgrims go to Varanasi to die and be cremated in the ghats that line the river. Their partially burned remains are dumped into the river, where you often see human body parts floating. The smell and noise and color of Varanasi was indelibly written in my mind…and NOW I had Ganges River water in my eyes. I was worried.

Morning dawns on the ghats at Varanasi.

Probably because of my worry, I felt that my eyes burned and stung. The guide assured me that the water was holy and no harm would come to me, but I was not so sure. I made up a lot of stories in my mind about how I would go blind from Ganges holy water.

Thankfully, in a few days I was fine and my vision, although not healed, returned to normal.

One moral to the above two stories is that, when you set intentions, you need to be very clear in the words that you use. Asking for clear vision, as I did, was not necessarily interpreted by the universe in the way that I meant it to be. So, when I suggest that you set intentions, remember to state them with full descriptiveness and be certain of what you want. Of course, I also believe that the Divine is much smarter than I am and will give me what I need...not necessarily what I think I need.

In 2010, we traveled to Cambodia and Vietnam. It was wonderful in many ways and challenging in several others. My biggest challenge was getting very sick about five days before returning home. Still, as with all of life, I learned many lessons from this experience.

I was and am amazed at the body's ability to know what it needs to heal. Whatever was wrong with me hit hard and fast and I went from feeling fine to feeling horrid in a matter of minutes. Then, as if someone had hit an off switch in my body, all I could do was sleep. For five days, except for the times when I had to get on a bus to move from one place to another, all I did was sleep. My body also refused to eat. I was very thirsty so I would drink a great deal of water, then fall back to sleep again. Apparently, my body was wise enough to know that water and sleep were what I needed to heal myself.

The illness hit just as we had arrived at Halong Bay, an amazingly beautiful bay filled with thousands of rock formations that rise eerily from the water and are engulfed in mist. It was one of the places I had really wanted to see, but there was simply no way I was able to take the boat trip to view the formations. I urged my husband and sister and brother-in- law to go, take pictures, and tell me all about it.

As I lay in bed that day though, it was as if a slide show was running in my brain, showing me flash after flash of the formations in a very fast sequence. I can't be sure what that was about, but I believe that the people who loved me and were seeing the scenery were somehow able to psychically transmit it back to me. Over the next few days, this happened again and again as my friends and family saw various sites.

Now, I assure you that I would much rather see with my physical eyes than through a slide show of projected visions. I also know some people might say I was hallucinating. I do, though, find it fascinating that our brains can view the world without the help of our physical eyes. I also realize as I write this that many of my travel lessons have to do with vision. I think that as long as I keep asking for clear vision I am likely to receive more than I expect. Travel lessons are like that.

One thing about lessons is that they are different for everyone. My students seem to always ask, "What does this MEAN?" Generally meanings are the least important of our lessons and they vary dramatically for each person, depending on what we need to learn. So Jean and I can take the same journey, attend the same ceremony, and do the same task, only to have totally different experiences. Here are some of Jean's lessons from experiencing worship, magic, and mystery in India and Bali.

We were so blessed to have ten days in Bali. Kathryn and I, with our spouses, based our day trips out of the crowded capital of Denpasar. Although we enjoyed the beach resorts and the humming tourist bustle of the city, Bali is such a spirit-filled adventure that we wanted to experience it all.

The Balinese have a unique view of the world. They view it as needing to contain equal parts of good and evil, light and dark, sorrow and joy. The Balinese people feel that it is their purpose in creation to maintain this balance in the world. They strive to embrace life in its totality.

Each Balinese temple is open on its anniversary and major holy days. Each village has at least one temple, so it is very hard to avoid a temple celebration while in Bali. All the hotels and newspapers publish the celebrations, and we were lucky enough to find that a Ngerebong, a celebration known for its trances, was occurring. Our driver followed a procession of women with huge displays of flowers and fruit (some weighing forty pounds) on their heads to the temple of Pura Petilan Pengerebongan.

It was stunningly, oppressively hot as we donned our sarongs and entered through the flag-bedecked temple portals. The temple itself is largely a big courtyard with covered pavilions and small shrines where offerings are placed. The temple complex was so crowded that people were standing ten deep all along the perimeter, there was barely room for a single person to walk between the two sides of the temple. The smell and press of the crowd was overwhelming. Nevertheless, the Balinese invited us to join them. I was soon adopted by a young man who explained everything to me in broken English. He was attending college and hoping to be a tour guide when he graduated. Everyone was laughing and insisting on having their photos taken with us. They were amazed that we were from America and not Australia. Bali is so close and cheap to visit that hordes of Aussies visit the island. They are not the most popular tourists with the local people.

After the villagers were blessed by the priests with holy water, grains of rice were placed on their foreheads, much like a Christian might have ashes on Ash Wednesday. The temple area had already been sanctified through the ritual bloodletting of cock fighting.

Suddenly the man in front of my husband yelped and began stabbing the air and himself with a Kris, a ceremonial knife. Although we were crowded tighter than sardines in a can, Fred immediately found a way to back away from the man. Quickly others from his village stepped up to escort the entranced man and keep him from hurting anyone. They all believed the knife would not pierce his own skin so he was not stopped from cutting himself. Several others around us also entered into a trance, and all were escorted around the temple three times.

Although several of the escorts did receive cuts, the entranced people continued to slash at their bodies without any evidence of injury or blood. "The gods have entered them," my young friend said in awe. "It is a great honor for them and their communities."

Eventually the priests roamed through the trancers and splashed them with holy water to bring them back to the world. It was far harder for us to return to that place we called reality.

Under a trance, this man stabs himself with a very sharp Kris.

The next day we were invited to the funeral of an eighty four-year-old woman. She was going to be cremated along with the bones of her husband who had died years before. In Bali the spirit is thought to linger until cremation releases it, so if one is buried the spirit may stay with the family until cremation.

The body was loaded into a woven palm-frond basket and carried to the cremation site on the shoulders of her four grandsons, who dipped and wove and turned in circles in an effort to confuse any evil spirits or ghosts that were attracted to the body.

When the cremation pyre was reached the body was placed in an ornate tower while a gamelan band played. She was surrounded by her belongings and gifts for the journey. Food, jewelry, teacups, fabric and a Hello Kitty purse were all piled on the pyre. A suckling pig and other food was prepared; the Balinese believe that the spirits consume the essence of the offerings but that the physical offering may be eaten by the living.

Again, we were welcomed with open arms to the party-like gathering. Everyone was having their photo taken in front of the pyre. Grandmother, four days dead in ninety-degree heat, was blessed by the priest and the gifts brought by others were given to her one by one. Live birds were released to fly the prayers to heaven.

Then the gifts were removed and the pyre lit. It was an amazing sight and smell to experience. Grandmother's body slipped part way through the cremation and she ended up with her feet pointing straight up. We were appalled and worried, but it was greeted with laughter by the family. The whole festivity was a joyful one as tears are thought to encourage the ghost to linger.

A cremation in Bali.

It was an amazing experience, and deeply spiritual. There is no disconnect from death with the Balinese, they feel it is but one stop on the wheel of life. The tower symbolizes the cosmos and the corpse is put in the middle of it to show its position between the spiritual and human worlds.

The ashes are taken to the sea in days to come. There, they believe, the soul passes through hell to be cleansed. The soul then is invited back to shore and the family temple where it resides until its next incarnation.

Our last experience with trance in Bali was at a temple trance dance. Two young girls (symbolizing holy angels) were put into a trance prior to the dance. We were told a divine spirit was believed to then inhabit them both simultaneously, and coordinate their actions as if they were one. With their eyes closed, they danced in perfect synchronicity, their movements coinciding completely. When they finished, sixty men clothed in black and white plaid sarongs (symbolizing the equality of light and dark) began to chant and clap. The sound was amazing, and I believe that we all entered a slight trance state ourselves. Suddenly a dancer had the horse spirit enter him and he pranced toward the bonfire. He stamped on it with his bare feet, dancing over the flames, even sitting on the fire at one point.

A priest eventually brought him out of the trance and he was unburned. It was an amazing and spiritual evening; the sounds of the chanters and the sight of the dancers in the flickering light of the fires were unforgettable.

These moments in Bali taught me more than I could have imagined. At first I was caught up in the novelty and glamour of the experiences, marveling that a girl from Pine City, Minnesota, could be part of a funeral procession in

Indonesia. The more I thought and wrote about the time there, the more I could see how profoundly my inner self had been listening.

I had the gift of being in a place where the holy was a part of every moment, not just a Sunday school lesson. Whether or not I fully believed that the woman standing next to me who went into a trance actually had a goddess enter her, I now DID believe that she had the power to slash at herself and do no harm. I had seen it.

What incredible power our beliefs hold. One can literally walk on fire or attune oneself with another to the point of sharing movement. The spark of the divine, the cosmos, God resides within us. Humans have used ritual and focusing meditations for millennia to quiet our rational minds and allow that spark to shine through into our mundane lives.

I started to look for, and find, the common threads in the worship ceremonies of many countries. Since I had grown up in a fundamentalist Christian community I was very familiar with that belief system. Now I searched for the sameness in different cultures. Was a sauna in Norway that far removed from a sweat lodge ceremony with the Lakota Indians? When a widow lit a candle in front of a photo of her husband and sighed, was it vastly different from placing an offering in a Shinto shrine to an ancestor? Were the Muslim prayer beads, the malas of the Buddhists, and the rosary of the Catholics not essentially the same?

India held the hardest challenges to my blossoming belief that the divine was present in all religions. From my childhood on, my most sacred moments were centered in quiet and reflection. In India it is IMPOSSIBLE to find silence. I exited the airport in Delhi to an unending cacophony of noise that never abated during the two weeks I was there. Even visually there is a noise that is unbelievable. There is always movement, color, animals, and people to challenge the eyes. There is no functioning on autopilot in India.

Of course, I wanted to visit as many Hindu temples as possible while learning more about their belief system. Usually when I enter any place of worship I feel a sense of calmness, a sigh of the sacred. Entering a Hindu temple was a different experience. Worshipers jumped up to ring a bell at the entrance, people pushed and prodded from every direction, talking and laughing as they approached the inner sanctum. Everywhere, accompanying the noise and movement, were the smells. A great deal of incense, rotting flower offerings, and the scent of unwashed humans joined with the odor of the rats and monkeys who wandered unimpeded through the temples. The statues and altars were as brightly colored as the saris of the women who left offerings at their bases. One is almost constantly reminded of the fertility and sexuality of the gods (something that was NOT encouraged in my Presbyterian Church of the 1960s).

I honestly struggled to find some way to relate to the Indian culture. My breaking point came as we toured an amazing old astronomical observatory in Jaipur with gorgeous marble and cooling breezes and very few visitors as the entrance fee was high. I felt myself relaxing and embracing India … then a stray dog walked by with a charred human hand in his mouth. I was more than ready to board the next flight back home!

Fortunately, I had nine more days to spend in India. As we drifted on the Ganges River at dawn, watching as people bathed and brushed their teeth in the same water that the partially cremated remains of their neighbors floated in, we tourists dropped small leaves with candles on them as tribute to the return of the sun and life. At that moment I began to understand that in India life was like a Mandala, that the circle brought both blessings and trials, that humanity was but a small part of this dance of life.

Our guide, Amit, was a member of an upper caste who had graduated from UCLA. He joyfully dipped his hands in the Ganges and offered to fill bottles of water for us to drink. He assured us that the water in this sacred river was totally safe, that it had been tested many times and was bacteria free. All of our guidebooks had said to avoid any contact with the Ganges water, as it was so toxic.

Amit then pointed to a beautiful three-story house on the bank of the river. "That is where my family lives," he said, "all eleven of us." I congratulated him, and said it was nice to have such a large house with a family of his size. "Oh," he said sadly, "it was very wonderful until the monkeys moved in. We used to have the three floors to live in, then they took the top floor. It was still acceptable as we had the two floors. But, just lately, it is very sad. They have taken over the second floor. So now all of us are living in just the three rooms on the main floor. We are very worried that the monkeys will push us out of even there. And the monkeys have made the house very dirty and smelly; we do not like it."

My husband, Fred, asked, "Why don't you just remove the monkeys?"

"No, no sir!" Amit replied, adamantly. "We are giving offerings to the monkeys and asking them to leave, but we cannot move them."

Fred and I talked at length that evening about the conversation and laughed that Amit, a college graduate, believed he had to give his house to the monkeys. As I lay in bed that night, listening to the honking taxis and unending buzz of Varanasi that drifted through the closed windows of our hotel, I began to wonder ... was my belief that I had the right to force nature and animals to do my bidding the correct one? Did I have the god-given right to eat other life forms, to take over wetlands and build on the prairies?

I still eat meat, I still live in a home without mice or monkeys. Now, though, I can question my belief system and at least contemplate that it may not contain the only answers. That is one of the true benefits of travel. It challenges one to come home and reexamine one's personal beliefs.

Look for the Divine in Unexpected Places

Occasionally I have challenged my students to an exercise that stretches their limits. I tell them to go to a place they would never go and look for the divine. When you travel, you often end up in places that are not of your choosing. At home, though, it takes more courage to walk into a place where you are not comfortable. One of my students, who knew she was rather judgmental about others, decided to go see what a strip club was all about. She was careful, bringing someone with her and going to a somewhat safe area, but she still told me that her heart was pounding almost out of her chest as she walked in the door and sat down, ordering a cola.

She laughingly reported that, at age fifty, she had seldom even entered a bar. So, for her, even the scent of stale beer was foreign. She also said that she was, in a way, disappointed that no one seemed shocked to see her there. She sat and drank her soda, watching a woman dancing. The woman seemed young and almost innocent, except for the way she was moving. My student was surprised to see a very small cross tattooed on the dancer's ankle. She decided to focus on the dancer's ankle instead of her toplessness and found that the longer she watched the more impressed she was with the dancer. A vision crossed her mind of watching a harem dancer in a past life. Perhaps, she thought, her judgment of this sort of thing was based on being a harem dancer in a past life. She reported on her field trip, as she called it, with a certain amount of humor. "Yes," she said to me, "there is, indeed, a piece of the sacred in everything."

If you wish to stretch yourself, you can do the same thing. Go to a place you would be unlikely to ever go. For me it might be a sporting event or a gambling casino. For my husband it would likely be a shopping mall or perhaps a New Age expo. It is interesting to ask yourself what places you would not commonly visit. Then, go to one with a sense of adventure and the eyes of a psychic wanderer and look for a hint of the divine. I am very certain you will find it.

One of my favorite quotes is "If anyone points out the moon to you and you see it, do you go on staring at the finger?" (Andrew Harvey). While this statement can be applied in many situations, it fits well to spiritual travel. In life in general, we often become so engrossed with the messenger that we sometimes forget to focus on the message. We are sometimes more interested in the broadcaster than we are in the news she is reporting or entranced with the minister but ignoring the sermon. When we travel, we sometimes focus so much on the storyline of places that we forget to see the place.

One of the functions of a good teacher of intuition or spirituality is to "point out the moon" and then get out of the way. We tend to focus on the way in which a message is delivered or on the person who is delivering it. This is how gurus, churches, dogmas, and political leaders are created. In the Christian tradition, this leads to the focus on church structure, ritual, and dogma instead of paying attention to the messages of Jesus. In more "new age" traditions, we sometimes follow gurus, teachers, and groups long after we have learned all they have to offer.

Becoming a psychic wanderer is like staring at the night sky and trying to make sense of the constellations. If you focus too much on labeling you run the risk of stepping out of the beauty and mystery of the stars. All of us are surrounded constantly with a huge volume of psychic messages. It is rather like swimming in a sea of information without knowing where you are going or what you want to know. The main function of a good teacher or guide is to show you how to focus on and interpret information so that you are not overwhelmed. The next function might just be to get out of the way.

The world is truly an amazingly beautiful, magical, and mystical place. I believe we came into this world to experience this, to stand in awe of earth's beauty and to learn joy. Perhaps our purpose in life really IS just that simple. Travel is one way to remember why we left the spirit realm and came to earth. The lessons learned on a physical trip are the same lessons we need to remember for all of life's journey.

chapter seven

If you cannot get rid of the family skeleton,
you may as well make it dance.
—GEORGE BERNARD SHAW

Shaking the Family Tree

Because I am a practicing psychic and medium, people assume I talk to my deceased loved ones on a regular basis. Actually, nothing could be further from the truth. With the exception of a goodbye, often said within a few days of their death, my relatives and friends who have passed on have been mostly silent to me. I am not disappointed about this. I have more than enough live people to pay attention to in my life and, once someone has died, I am patient enough to wait until I join them in the spirit realm to talk to them again.

Strangely, the two most vivid experiences of speaking to my deceased relatives both happened in a foreign country. By now, you should not be surprised by this. As we have discussed several times, the act of traveling puts us in a state of mind where mystical experiences are much more likely to occur. This is especially true if you happen to be traveling to a country where your family roots originate.

I believe that our bodies themselves resonate with the soil of the places we live and have lived. We leave a type of psychic or vibratory trace that stays with the land even after we have left it. Indigenous peoples know this, often honoring the places where their ancestors trod long after they have ceased to live on that land. In Western countries, though, we tend to honor our loved ones at the places they are buried, rather than where they lived. Remains do, in my experience, have a vibration and memory, but I would much rather visit a family home or other place the loved one frequented, than a cemetery where his or her bones are laid.

Returning to our familial roots can answer many questions and heal old wounds. Visiting a home where you used to live, a school you used to attend, or the country where your ancestors were born can provide amazing healing, especially when done while using your third eye.

It is no wonder that traveling back to the lands of their ancestors has caused many people to have mystical and intuitive experiences. I think that is one of the reasons that so many people do genealogy as well. It not only teaches them who they have been, it also shows them who they could be.

In 2006 the foreign rights to my book, *The Intuitive Advantage*, were purchased by a publishing company in the Netherlands and I was thrilled when they asked me to go over to Holland for a promotional tour and book signing. They were able to set up an event in the small town of Winterswijk, where my father had been born almost a hundred years earlier and from which he had emigrated in 1920.

Jean was able to go with me and we also contacted several Dutch cousins of the Harwig branch who helped arrange a family reunion for us. The town is quite small, so the book signing at a local booksellers was a major occasion, especially since I was considered to be a hometown girl, returning after a long absence. So, the bookstore was packed and a cousin I had just met was translating my English talk into Dutch.

The bookstore gave me flowers and the local radio and newspaper covered the event. I likely will never feel so famous again. Then, as I stood to speak, I had an overwhelming sense of my father. I knew he was standing behind me, a huge smile of pride on his face. I could feel his joy that his daughter had returned to his birthplace, reunited with relatives, and that his last name was on the cover of a book written in his native language.

I choked up, almost unable to speak as the emotions flooded through me. Then, I felt his supportive hand on my shoulder, as real as any physical sensation could be. The tears in my eyes dried and I was able to speak and address the group. Dad was able to lift me up and give me the courage it took to speak from my heart, even though I had never learned the Dutch language.

My parents had always wanted us to go with them to Europe, but my husband and I were newly married, working, and then finishing law school. I had always thought we would go someday but, unfortunately, that day never came while they were alive. Jean's and my father died unexpectedly of a heart attack in 1984 and our mother went the same way in 1988. I had always been disappointed that they did not get to see that I went on to write books. I had also felt guilty that we had put off traveling with them. Then, on that night in Winterswijk,

I realized that of course they knew I was an author and that I was, indeed, able to travel with them now.

Something in me healed that night. I no longer felt guilty about being unable to say goodbye, go back with my dad to his fatherland or show off my newest book to my parents. I realized in a very real way that I could still do those things...even if they were physically dead.

Could I have learned those lessons at a book signing in my hometown? Yes, of course, but it is likely they would not have been as vivid or as life changing. The circumstances of being in my father's hometown invited his spirit to pay attention to me and it allowed me the time and setting to be able to process my emotions and insights.

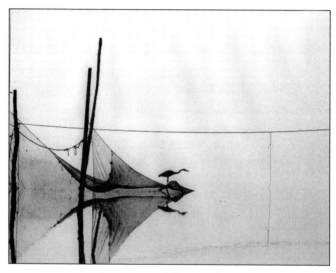

A crane on a dyke in Holland

Going Home Exercise

Perhaps you can't return to your family's roots by way of going to a foreign land, but you can return to your own personal roots and see who shows up to say hello. It is, of course, just as possible for your deceased mother to speak to you in your own bedroom as it is if you return to your childhood home. You are far more likely to focus on her, ask her to visit with you, and pay attention to what happens, though, if you are in a place that reminds you of her.

Talking to spirits is, like most of intuitive work, about focusing and paying attention. It is good to go into it with no expectations. You might not hear a voice in your head or see an image. You might get a whiff of cigar smoke and realize it is your father's favorite cigar scent. You could find a penny on the sidewalk just when you were wishing your mother was there to give you financial advice. A butterfly might land on your hand, giving a blessing of love from a favorite aunt. You might suddenly hear a song on the radio or in your mind. All of these are used by spirits as a way to communicate with us. Be open to accept whatever happens to you as a message from your loved one.

Start by going to a place that you and the loved one have shared such as your family home, a restaurant you both enjoyed, maybe even a park where you used to go for picnics. If it is not possible to go to a physical place, you can also just sit quietly and visualize the place where you wish to go. Then, fix a mental image of the person you want to communicate with in your mind and ask the person a question. You might also want to bring a photograph of the person and focus on that. Keep your mind focused on the mental or photographic image of the person you want to communicate with but do not put words in his mouth. Wait patiently for the reply.

You will get a reply but it may not come in the way that you expect it to come. Accept whatever appears and interpret it according to your intuition. If you need clarification, it is fine to ask more questions. Treat the experience as a true conversation with your loved one and expect surprising answers. Enjoy this experience and feel the love that will fill you as you bless the spirit with the honor of the conversation. It is wonderful to discover that you are never really alone. Spirits want and love to talk to us, just as we long to speak with them.

It is fascinating to watch people transform when they visit a country where they have family roots. My group trips tend to be to places that are very exotic and seldom to places where the participants' ancestors originated. Recently, though, I led a group of spiritual travelers to Ireland. At least half of the group had some family origins there or a grandparent or great-grandparent who had immigrated to the United States from Ireland. Part of their motivation for joining this trip was to see their ancestral homeland and to feel their roots. It was interesting to see how at home they were in this new country. Many of them commented on how familiar everything felt. They liked the food, drank lots of Guinness and didn't complain that it was rainy and chilly all the time. I could almost watch the tension drip away as their bodies relaxed into a country that seemed liked home to them, even if they had never been there before.

I have no Irish heritage and realized that it was a very different trip for me than it was for them. I DID complain about the weather. I looked at things with a traveler's eye rather than that of a pilgrim returning to her roots. They looked at things and saw home. Even after they returned to the United States, many of them told me they felt more comfortable in their bodies and more at home with who they were. They had, in a small way, recovered a part of themselves that they hadn't known was missing.

One of the participants, Jill, had recently lost her brother and was grieving him and some other losses in her life. Here is her description of how she found peace and clarity by returning to her roots.

"From the time I was a little girl, listening to the stories my Grandpa Harry told about his family who came from Ireland, I have wanted to go to Ireland and walk in the footsteps of my family. I have wanted to breathe the air that they did and feel the earth in my fingers that they felt and see the mists on the mountains and the heather on the hillsides that they saw. My dream of visiting the land of my ancestors, Ireland, came true in September 2011, on a trip with Kathryn and our guide, Finbarr Ross. After starting with one driver, and ending with a third one, Kevin, on the third or fourth day, we were set for the rest of the trip. When we arrived outside County Cork, I asked Kevin if there would be a sign that said Cork that we could stop at and take a picture and a place where we could stop and get some dirt from County Cork for my brother's grave. He told me of course there would and when we got to the sign, he stopped and I had my picture taken by the sign. The dirt I sort of forgot about with all of the excitement of seeing places, going to the pubs with Kevin and the group and shopping. The day we were leaving Cork, Kevin came up to me with a small sack of dirt and told me, per my request, that here was the dirt I requested from County Cork for my brother Raymond's grave back home in the U.S. I had become very fond of Kevin, he had become like my Irish brother. Perhaps there was even a family connection in a past life. So, it was my Irish brother, Kevin, procuring dirt for the grave of my blood brother, Raymond, back home. I believe that my brother in spirit might have had something to do with Kevin becoming our driver. Before I made the decision to sign on for the trip, I went to my brother's grave and asked him what I should do. What I heard was, "Go for the both of us." That the trip was divinely inspired I have no doubt, from all that I experienced, learned, and felt. As I sprinkled the dirt upon my brother's grave I said, "I'm ready for whatever is asked of me."

Jean and I had our own amazing and healing experience in Turkey, many years ago. Like Jill, we had experienced a death in the family and found peace in an unexpected place. Here is how Jean describes it:

> Our oldest sister had died very unexpectedly about two years before our family trip to Turkey. Her two children, my brother and sister, and our spouses had all made the commitment to spending time together while remembering and celebrating Ruth. She had always wanted to travel, but never had taken the time and money to do so. It felt right to have this celebratory adventure in her honor.
>
> Turkey has more Greek and Roman ruins than either Greece or Italy. This day we headed out to Sardis and toured the city that King Croesus had lived in. The Sardis ruins were in a lovely valley surrounded by hills that seemed to be temples themselves.
>
> I asked our guide if we were far from an old worship site about which I had read. He assured us that while it

would only take a few minutes to see the Temple of Artemis that was located close by, it really was not worth touring. Wouldn't we rather go shopping?

Still, when we insisted, he agreed to take us there.

Our van climbed up into the hills under the incredible blue skies of Turkey. As we looked down into the valley it seemed that a sea of windflowers, daisies, and anemones were paving the way down to the Temple. We parked the vehicle and walked under olive trees that had their own presence; many of them were over a thousand years old and emitting a sense of deep calm.

The remains of this temple to the goddess of wisdom were amazing. The power of the place was apparent, even to the noisiest of our tourist companions, and soon everyone was sitting in the sunshine and soaking up Diana's healing powers. Kathryn and I picked some wild flowers and walked to the center of the temple complex. There we left our offerings.

I was filled with a knowing that this was where we could release our grief and ties to the sadness that surrounded our sister's death. I whispered to Kathryn to let Ruthie go, she was happy now. Both of us looked up and saw her spirit dancing by the altar. Our niece slipped her hand in mine, our nephew put an arm about Kathryn. Healing tears were shed.

As we walked back to the van, Kathryn and I compared notes, surprised that we had both seen Ruth dancing (something she was not known for in life) and more surprised that we both saw her wearing the same outfit. At the same moment we both picked feathers off the path, laughed and said, "Ruthie?" We blew the feathers to the wind and watched them drift away.

There is no doubt in my mind that Ruth stood with us in that temple in Turkey, that the spirit of the divine feminine still emanated and allowed us to heal our little family in a way that no funeral ceremony could have. Of course, we could have designed a formal ritual or had a church service ... but the gift of travel is that often we will stumble across the exact place and moment that we need.

The temple of Artemis in the hills of Turkey.

You don't, of course, need to go to Holland or Turkey or Ireland to experience these types of connections with your deceased loved ones. While travel does seem to make people more amenable to spirit communication, spirits are not limited to time or space. They can visit you in your backyard or a local park and are often around places such as former homes, schools and even workplaces.

None of my family has any genetic roots to Turkey and yet the experience there with Ruthie was one of my strongest and most powerful spirit encounters. So, if you want to experience healing from a death or need a message of comfort from a loved one who has passed, going to a beautiful place and feeling the energy may, in fact, call them to you. It is your openness and willingness to experience the divine that will bring the connection to you. It is also your ability to suspend your disbelief and engulf yourself in the sensation. For a minute, at least, try not to think, "Am I making this up?"

Of course what happened to my family in Turkey could have been coincidences or imagination. I don't believe so, however. I judge what is true based on how it affects me. All the healings we have written about above affected me and others in a positive, concrete way. That is proof enough for me.

Often, spirit communication and intuitive messages come to us in the form of dreams.

One of the most amazing intuitive dream experiences I have ever witnessed happened in Germany when my husband, Loren, and I were on a genealogical search for his family roots. He knew that the Magsams (his family name) were from a certain part of Germany, but other than that we had little to go by, so we were stopping at various churches and courthouses looking for grave markers and historical records. We weren't having much luck but we were enjoying seeing the country, trying the local food, and staying in zimmers (usually a room in someone's house that they rented out to travelers).

A practice that Loren and I have gotten into after many years of marriage is that we often tell the other of dreams that we had the night before. It is a fun breakfast conversation and usually gives us both insights into things that are causing us concern or just a good laugh at how absurd dreams can be.

All of us dream nightly, although some people claim not to. I find that my dreams when I travel tend to be even more vivid and meaningful than they usually are. One night on that trip to Germany, Loren had an amazing dream.

When he told it to me over breakfast, we both just had a laugh at the unusualness of the dream. He had dreamed that we were walking in a German cemetery located on the grounds of a church. This was not at all surprising, of course, since we had already done that several times on that trip. What WAS unusual is that in his dream he had found a pile of broken grave markers at the corner of the cemetery. He told me that he had gone to the pile and started digging, certain that this was where he would find his ancestors. Instead, he related, he only found a marker for a man named Andresen.

We had laughed at the dream, both saying that the name meant nothing to either of us. Our interpretation was that since he was searching for his roots, digging in a pile of broken and discarded markers was a sign that he was feeling a bit discouraged in his quest, especially since the one he found in the dream was not a Magsam.

After breakfast we headed off again and, sure enough, ended up at a church cemetery. As we turned a corner of the church we were both shocked to see a pile of discarded and broken grave markers, exactly as Loren had seen in his dream.

Loren went to the pile, looked down, and there, on the very top of the pile, lay the exact same marker that he had seen in his dream. It was the marker with the last name of a man named Andresen, precisely as he had dreamed it the night before.

I think we were both a bit shaken at receiving proof of Loren's prophetic dream. He looked for a bit longer, finding as expected, NO Magsam tombstones in the pile. We researched the name when we got home but were never able to find any family connection to the man whose name was on the marker. We did, however, find out that piles of broken markers are not uncommon in Germany.

After we returned home, Loren did some computer research and learned that in Germany and some other European countries the burial plots are rented for a period of years, not purchased as we do in the United States. So, if the family doesn't renew the lease when it expires, the grave markers are uprooted and tossed into a pile, often just in a corner of the cemetery. There they break and deteriorate unless claimed by a family member. Loren insists that he did not know this fact before having his dream and so could not imagine why there would ever be a pile of broken grave markers anywhere. Still, his intuitive mind DID know…and led him to explore this avenue. It also gave us both concrete proof that intuitive dreams do occur, right down to giving a name!

How to do dream work

Doing dream work is a wonderful addition to any traveling you might do, whether a weekend vacation to a round the world journey. It also is a great way to get intuitive messages at home. If you want to do this, it is important to have a topic or question that you would like to dream about. That way you will be better able to interpret the dream the next day. If Loren had asked for a certain dream topic, we might have been better able to interpret his grave marker dream.

If you are a person who claims not to dream, be aware that all people dream and that you generally have three or more dream periods every night. You DO dream, your task is to recall the dreams with clarity.

In order to do that, you should first set your intention upon going to bed. Perhaps you want some information about why you came to a certain destination or how your travels will go the next day. Whatever your question, tell yourself that you will have an intuitive dream about that topic that evening, that you will momentarily awaken after the dream, and that you will remember it.

The key to remembering your dreams is to not move until you have transferred the dream into your conscious mind. When you awaken from a dream, don't turn over or sit up. Allow yourself to lie comfortably as you review the dream in your consciousness, going over all the details. At this point, don't analyze the dream; just commit the details to memory. Then, if possible write the dream down. Some people keep a pen and paper by the bedside for this purpose. I prefer to trust that I will remember it, review it in my mind, fall back to sleep, and write it down the next day.

The next step in the process is to determine if the dream is an intuitive dream or a psychological dream. Most of our dreams are psychological. Our brain uses our dreamtime to process issues, dump feelings, and give us insights into our behavior. These dreams are very useful when it comes to dealing with emotional issues. Analyzing these dreams can be very valuable, but they are not the dreams we are looking for now. We are dealing only with intuitive dreams.

So how do you know the difference? First of all, psychological dreams usually have strong emotions attached to them. You may wake up frightened, angry, or crying. Also, the content of psychological dreams usually has some relationship to what you are currently experiencing or feeling in your life. If you are frustrated at work, for example, you might have a dream where you are lost in a tunnel and don't know which way to turn.

Intuitive dreams have a very different feeling to them. Even though the content might be disturbing, you tend to wake up very peaceful and passive after an intuitive dream. You know on some level that the content wasn't about real time events, but rather a message given to you with that particular symbolism. Intuitive dreams feel important, but not emotional.

For the sake of this exercise, trust yourself to know the difference. The more you ask for intuitive dreams, the more your brain will supply them to you. Don't be disappointed if you aren't sure. Just use the dream you are given.

Interpreting intuitive dreams is not as complex as many people make it out to be. After all, you are intuitive and it is your dream. When you have an intuitive dream, you should ask yourself this: "What do these symbols and messages mean to me in regard to the question I asked the night before?" Your intuition will give you the correct interpretation. Dream interpretation books are, in my opinion, of little value. The interpretation of a symbol or happening is up to you. Snakes are scary for some people, sacred to others, and a sign of healing for some. How to interpret a snake or any other symbol is up to your feelings in regard to it.

Trust your intuition to tell you what you need to know. Then take the information you receive and use it in your life. Even if you are on a trip, the information is very likely to be something that will help your life when you get home. Plus, you are gaining valuable practice in a technique that will serve you well, wherever you may be.

chapter eight

*My life often seemed to me like a story
that has no beginning and no end.*

—CARL JUNG

Discovering Your Past Lives on Your Wanderings

As a psychic, one of the most common questions asked of me is, "Why am I here? What is my life's purpose?" Many people feel that they have come to earth to fulfill a purpose. Most of us are overflowing with questions that we don't know how to answer. We have character traits that seem purposeful and which we can't seem to change, even if we want to do so. We meet and enter relationships with the same type of person over and over again. We are drawn to certain jobs or hobbies, even though no one else in our family or acquaintance has the least interest in them. Many of us long to travel to a certain place or feel comfortable in areas we have never been before in this lifetime. All of these are signs of past-life influences that are still present in your life. There are as many reasons to travel as there are pilgrims on the road, but one of the reasons we journey is to try to answer a few of those questions.

If you travel long enough, you are bound to come upon places where you feel a sense of déjà vu. Déjà vu is a French term that literally means "already seen." It is an overwhelming sense of familiarity with something that shouldn't be familiar at all. Say, for example, you are traveling to Europe for the first time. Perhaps you are touring a castle and suddenly it seems as if you have been in that very spot before. You may even know the layout of the rooms without having any possible way of knowing that. Another example closer to home could be meeting a person for the first time and entering into a conversation, only to have the feeling that you've already experienced that very conversation—same person, same place, same topic.

Déjà vu, in my opinion, stems from the fact that we all have lived on this planet many times, usually accompanied by a core group of loved ones and others with whom we have contracted to fulfill a purpose. Going to a particular place will often trigger a past-life memory, that, in turn, can help us figure out our current life's purpose and perhaps explain more about certain relationships. I also believe we are drawn to travel to certain places because we long to return to a familiar place or to relive the scene of a crime where something significant occurred to us.

Some surveys indicate that as high as 70 percent of the population has experienced some type of déjà vu. It is a gift, I believe, to help us know who we are and why we are here.

Many years ago I traveled with a group to Thailand. I fell immediately and completely in love with the country and especially, as I called them, all the Buddha boys. This very irreverent term was my nickname for the young Buddhist monks that are a common sight throughout Thailand. Thai men are not considered to be mature adults until they have become monks for a period of time, so almost every male becomes a monk ... some for just a few months and some for the rest of their life.

Young Cambodian monks enjoying our visit with them.

Every time I saw a Buddha boy I smiled a lot. They just made me happy. When we went to see the ruined city of Ayut-thaya in Thailand, I realized why. Ayutthaya was a huge capital city, founded in the 1300s and destroyed in the 1700s. All that remains now are ruins and memories. Many of the temples remain semi-intact and still have a small number of monks and nuns that attend them. The minute I walked into the ruins of the temples I felt at home. I knew, without being able to say how, the exact layout of the temple grounds. I felt as if I could have led a tour. "This," I wanted to say, "is where we slept and this is where we ate and, oh my, this statue is really not in the right place at all." It felt peaceful and oh, so familiar.

I am certain that at some point in my life I was a Buddhist monk at Ayutthaya. I think I was no one of importance, yet that life has colored my current one. Even today I have an affinity for statues of the Buddha (Thai statues, mostly) and I am happiest when I have a great deal of solitude and quiet. Being physically present in Ayutthaya explained these yearnings for me in a way that allows me to honor those parts of who I am.

That is really the value of past-life memories. They explain, in a visceral way, why we act and feel the way we do in THIS life. With that knowledge, we can make free choices about whether we wish to embrace those parts of who we are … or decide that they no longer suit us.

Jean had a similar experience when she visited Egypt. Here is how she describes it:

> When I was a little girl one of my earliest memories is having my grandmother very upset with me. I was insisting that I had lived in Egypt and could not eat fish, that only very poor people ate fish. I stole my sister's eyeliner and applied it with a heavy hand, saying that I was a queen. My grandparents had a coffee table book with photographs of the world. I would sneak it into the spare bedroom and spend hours looking at the color photographs of Thebes and Cairo. Then I would happily tell everyone stories about Egypt and my life there. Finally, around age five, I was forcefully told to quit telling lies about this past life.

Egypt was a fixation and a love of mine all throughout my life. I traveled from Minneapolis to Chicago by bus to see the King Tut exhibit in the late 1970s, working extra shifts waitressing and skipping college classes to get there.

When the chance to go to Egypt came, I was overcome with expectations. I truly expected the entire country to be my home, that it would resonate with me to my core.

Instead, I felt ... nothing. Our first day at the pyramids I was so disappointed. As others felt mystical vibes and celebrated their connection to the cosmos I sat outside the tombs and wondered what the fuss was about. Cairo was a big, ugly city full of noise and pollution. The sphinx was tiny. The desert was dusty.

I absolutely adored every monument and tomb we saw, but it was with a historian's and artist's eye. I had seen and studied so much about Egypt and all the different dynasties, it was amazing to see these things in person. But I did feel strangely cheated that there was no deeper connection, no sense of familiarity.

Then we boarded our cruise boat and the Nile worked her magic. As I sat alone on the upper deck and watched the timeless scenery I suddenly was transported back to a past I remembered. In my mind's eye, I watched hippos at the shore and celebrated the old villages as we drifted by.

We docked at a very small and seldom visited temple, Edfu, for the evening. I immediately felt more at peace than I had for years, and my sleep was deep and dreamless. Entering the temple the next morning brought the knowledge that I had lived here. The years passed away and the frescoes were colored vividly. I could smell the incense and papyrus.

I needed to leave the guide as I thought he was talking such nonsense and giving out so many incorrect facts. Slipping away I wandered to the very back of a small corridor, where there was a room only 20 feet by 24 feet or so. I could feel the cooler air brush my knees (although I was wearing long pants) and hear the swish of the loin cloth tied at my waist. Again I could smell incense and heard a murmur of chanting from another area. The room was filled with scrolls and low tables, and several other scribes were there reading.

Moments later the guide, Walid, caught up with me, chastising me for leaving his tour. No, no, there was no library. This was a temple and this would have been an altar area, he said.

Again I left Walid and kept exploring on my own, eventually finding the curator of the site. As I asked questions he opened up more and more, seeing that I wanted more than the surface information. He was quite excited when I asked about scrolls, and hurriedly escorted me back to the room I had left earlier. Edfu was rare in that it had housed a library within the temple walls. We walked to the room across the hall together, and I was overwhelmed with the smells of perfumes. I asked the curator if this was where perfumes were made, and he told me that yes, indeed, this was where the Goddess Hathor was anointed with unguents and various ointments were mixed. Archeologists had found many bottles and a laboratory for the preparation of perfumes when the temple had been rediscovered.

This temple, Edfu, was where the Goddess Hathor traveled once each year matching the cycle of the Nile to meet with Horus, the Falcon God. Here the great meeting took place and Egypt was made fertile again. I can only tell you that I have always felt a great affinity for the raptors, and have been given the name of Eagle Hawk Woman by a Lakota elder. Seeing the statues of Horus, the falcon god, again filled my spirit. As tourists lined up to have their photos taken beside a life-sized statue of Horus, I looked up. There, high above us in the blue sky, were two soaring falcons.

I was home.

The hawk god, Horus, at Edfu.

Of course, you don't have to travel to Thailand or Egypt to experience past-life memories. Sometimes, your memories will be prompted by the type of places that feel like home to you. For example, people who are drawn to live on water or in the woods or in cities might very well feel that affinity because many of their lives were lived in those surroundings.

Where do you feel most comfortable?

Take a moment to sit quietly and let your mind give you a picture of where you feel most comfortable. Is there water? If so, is it a lake, river, or ocean? Are you in the woods or in a big city? Are there buildings? If so, what do they look like? Are you alone or in the midst of a bustling crowd? All these are clues of a location where you might have lived in a former life.

Now let your mind's eye look down at your body. What are you wearing? What color is your skin? Look at your feet. Are you barefoot? Wearing sandals or perhaps elegant heels? What sex are you … what age? Trust the images that appear in your mind and simply believe that you are being given a glimpse of yourself as you once were.

This is a valuable exercise to apply to your current life. Try to incorporate some elements from your vision into your home. You might not be able to live on the water but you can have a small fountain in your living area. Perhaps you could add a houseplant or a small statue to your decorating. Maybe you need to go barefoot more often or wear silk on occasion. If you feel an affinity with a certain country or region, put a photo of that area on a shelf or desk. Adding back even tiny elements of a former life will make you feel more whole, complete and at home.

Whenever you feel a profound sense of being home you might be flooded with memories and emotions that seem not to make sense. Rather than discounting them, allow yourselves to experience them and see if a "story" is given to you. It is highly likely that you are being told something that you need to know.

Our brother Jim had such an experience while sitting on the shore of Lake Superior, not far from where he now lives. As Jean writes:

My brother and I sat on the shoreline of Lake Superior, the moon slowly rising over her tranquil waters. Jim had recently bought an apartment in Minneapolis and his job was going well, earning him a promotion and chances for more work-related travel. Life seemed to be on track for him, but there was still a sense that he was not happy.

We chatted about how well life was going until the quiet worked its magic, and our mundane subjects turned to the more profound. Eventually we sat in silence as the stars came out. Suddenly Jim was crying. He explained to me that as he sat there, listening to nature and his heart, he had a clear vision of himself on a sailing vessel pulling into a small port town. At that moment he knew that his happiness lay in living on the water.

I truly believe that short past-life memory and experience with the divine guided him to his present life. Jim was not aware consciously, perhaps, but every step he took led to the life he has now. He resolved a life-long health issue, losing two hundred pounds along the way. He actively started pursuing joy and fell in love with a woman from the small town of Grand Marais, Minnesota. He realized that a small urban apartment and stressful corporate routine was not for him.

Within two years he was living on the shores of Lake Superior, Minnesota's inland sea, and was finally home. Now, he may not be on the fast track to success in the big city, but I believe that his weekend getaway to Duluth saved his life. By taking a few days to escape the busyness and listen to his inner guides he found his path. Travel removed him from his routine and provided the spiritual space for him to hear his soul speak.

Was it a past-life remembrance of sailing the Mediterranean? That was what we talked of that night, his vivid moment of remembering what it felt like to be at sea. Or was it just his soul expressing his deepest longing?

I think it doesn't really matter. When we asked Jim if we could include his story in our book, here is what he said:

"I still remember that evening very clearly, it wasn't like a dream or my imagination. I quite literally saw myself in a tunic. I looked down at my feet and saw sandals tied up to my knees, on my hip was a short sword. I knew absolutely that I was standing out looking at the full moon somewhere on a pier in a port in the Mediterranean ... I absolutely knew it as if I was physically there.

"I do believe that there has been a cosmic force, name it what you will, moving me. All the things I used to think that would make me happy ended up almost killing me, while the things I never wanted ... responsibility, wife, daughter, small town life, are now the very things that make me the most content. It's very odd to me how important it is for me to be needed. I spent half a lifetime fleeing responsibility and now it is one of the things I am most proud of ... people can count on me."

Sometimes, unfortunately, the memories that arise in a past-life experience are not always pleasant. We live, after all, in a world where awful things happen to people. Still, remembering unpleasant and even violent happenings can also aid you in your current life.

A few years back I led a group of spiritual seekers to some of the Mayan cities of the Yucatan. We were touring Chichen Itza, a large Mayan ruin near Cancun, Mexico, when one of the women in our group fell to her knees, sobbing and moaning.

Our group was standing on the edge of a cenote, a deep natural pit or sinkhole, that are very common in that part of Mexico. Mary's (name changed) collapse was rather dramatic, but most of the people in our group were not overly concerned. We were used to people having strong responses to various sites. We held her hand and let her cry, knowing it was part of her journey.

Suddenly a security guard of the site ran up, very concerned that she was ill. He wasn't at all convinced when we told him she would be fine. I am certain, to be honest, that he thought we were being cruel to just let her sob and writhe. Then, after a number of minutes, Mary returned to her normal self and explained what had happened to her.

She had experienced a strong past-life vision of being thrown into the cenote as a sacrifice to the Mayan gods. Her terror had been as real as if it was happening to her that day. The guard listened to her tale, shaken now himself. Yes, he said, they had found many skeletons at the bottom of the cenote. They were believed to be of victims who had been sacrificed and were primarily female. The site didn't publicize that as they didn't wish to make it a focal point of the ruin complex.

Mary emerged from the experience shaken and yet grateful. All of her life she had been afraid of becoming a victim of violence. Now that she had experienced her sacrifice in a past life, she also saw it for what it was. She knew it was a past-life memory, not a current life issue. In some way, she left the ruins much stronger than when she arrived.

That is the thing with past-life memories. They change your perception of current life issues. The best way to be prompted to remember them is to be in a place that triggers the memories on an unconscious level. The prompt can be a smell, a sound, a sight or a feeling, but it will feel different... absolutely real. Traveling is a wonderful way to experience this delightful phenomenon but it can also happen through watching television or movies, going to museums, or reading a book.

Sometimes, past-life memories can be triggered not by a place but by a person. My most vivid experience with that occurred at the Incan ruins of Pachacamac. Pachacamac is a little-visited archaeological site about twenty five miles south of Lima, Peru. I was leading a tour of mystical seekers and Pachacamac was not on the itinerary. Actually, I had never even heard of it. However, through a series of rather bizarre events, it was where I had my most unusual past-life experience.

Days before, my group had been on the train to Machu Picchu when one of my fellow traveler's bags was stolen. Unfortunately, her passport, camera, credit cards, and money were all in the same bag. Other than a major illness or injury, losing a passport is just about the worst thing that can happen to a traveler in a foreign country because you can't leave the country without it.

We were due to fly home in three days and were told that it is rare to even get a replacement passport in that length of time. We were informed that we had to apply for it immediately and in person if she had any hope of catching her flight home. The closest American embassy was in Lima so Sheryl and I had to leave the group, fly to Lima and go to the embassy as soon as possible.

Sheryl was, of course, without ID, money, or credit cards, so we were both operating on a shoestring financially—on what money I had left and on a timeline (trying to get the passport in time for her to fly home). Miraculously, everything fell neatly into place in record time. We spent a day at the American embassy, watching as what everyone said could not be done was in fact done, and then had a free day before we were reunited with the rest of group and headed home.

We certainly didn't wish to spend our last day in Peru sitting around a hotel, but we had very little money and Lima is a huge and quite dangerous city for two women alone. Not letting that stop us, we rented a cab with our last bit of funds and asked the driver to take us to whatever ruins happened to be nearby.

An hour or so later he brought us to Pachacamac. Compared to Machu Picchu or other popular and breathtaking sites in Peru, Pachacamac was a disappointment. It had been a major site of the Incans but erosion has worn away most of the buildings and much of the site has yet to be uncovered. Still, as soon as we got out of the cab we both felt a sense of peace and excitement. Sheryl and I each felt that we had been led to that site by unseen forces.

Unlike the more major sites, Pachacamac was almost deserted. After paying a small admission fee we were met by a young Peruvian man who volunteered to guide us through the site. The minute his eyes met mine I realized that I knew him … completely and totally knew him. He and I walked through the site as if we were old friends walking around our hometown. Strangely, I remember very little about the ruins or buildings. All I remember is how comfortable I was in the presence of that man and how much he seemed to feel the same way. It felt, to me as if he and I had been transported to another time when we were a couple.

The interesting thing about this story is that Sheryl watched it unfold. Later, when we discussed it, she said that she felt as if she was an observer, watching a reunion of old friends or lovers. She described it as watching a movie where he and I were in a type of bubble where time and space no longer existed. She insists that she didn't feel like an outsider, but rather as if she was observing something rare and unusual. Our guide, I believe, was a young guard whom I had fallen in love with in that lifetime but whose love was not permitted to a temple oracle.

Then, when we arrived at a place we later learned was the site of the residence of the oracles, both Sheryl and I had a clear feeling and picture of having been there together as sister oracles. The grounds of the ruin had not seemed as familiar to her because often the young oracles were not allowed to leave their quarters. We held hands as we gazed at our former dwelling place, finally understanding why we had become such close friends in this lifetime. Since the minute Sheryl and I met, many years before this trip, we have felt a close and comfortable friendship. No wonder we were led back to Pachacamac to see our old living quarters!

I don't really have an explanation for what happened that day between me and the guide. I only know that our age and nationality differences disappeared and that all that was left were two dear friends who had always been together. Then, as we returned to the front gate, just as quickly he became a young Peruvian guide and I became a middle-aged American tourist. We tipped him and left.

I think most people have had an experience with meeting someone who they feel connected to on a deep level even though they have only just met. In this case the site seemed less of a trigger than the person. I believe that everything that happened up to that point ... the lost passport, the cab driving us out of town ... was meant to be so that I could experience the phenomena of traveling back in time with one close friend and then meeting another. Sheryl believes that her role was to come along to observe it, verify to me that it was real, and learn that time, space, and relationships are not quite as solid as we have been led to believe. Once again, she was working as a sister to me.

Past-Life Visualization exercise

You don't have to travel abroad to remember past lives or to get advice about how they are affecting you today. Here is a visualization that you can do anywhere. It may not be as powerful and unexpected as a spontaneous past-life recall, but it is just as valuable.

Set the intention that you are going to experience a visualization of a past life. Don't worry if you feel you are just making it up, as imagination is a part of intuition. Also, if you don't visualize well, just intend that you will get words or a story that you will hear in your head.

Have a piece of paper or two nearby on which to write. Then, use a relaxation exercise such as the one of loosening your tongue or watching your breath or some other technique you may like to use and then tell yourself you going on a journey to a place you have always been intrigued by or wanted to go to, or perhaps have visited because you are so drawn by it. This place can be another country, a section of this country, or even a place that no longer exists (e.g. Atlantis) or is out of this world (e.g. Mars). Don't agonize about the place, just take the first place that pops into your mind. This place should be as specific as possible (for example, Paris, Sedona, ancient Greece, etc.). Write this place down on your piece of paper.

Next, close your eyes and go to this place in your mind's eye. When you get there, intend to be met by a person or being. Trust that a person or being will appear in your vision or the thought of this being will come to your mind. Put aside the idea that you are making this all up and spend a few minutes in the presence of this person or being, perhaps having a conversation. Do not attempt to press or control the conversation and, when you feel finished, come out of the visualization and write as much as you can about who the person was and what was said. Perhaps you will even have a name, but that is really not important. Write, in as great detail as possible, everything you can remember to describe the person and most importantly describe the being's personality. Also, make notes of what the person said to you, again in as much detail as possible.

After you are done writing, go back to the visualization. Each time you come in and out of a relaxed trace state, it will be easier to reenter it at will. In your mind's eye, return to the same location, but this time you will take some action. As you visualize, ask yourself what you are now DOING. After sitting for a few moments watching yourself act, open your eyes and write down, as specifically as you can, exactly what you were doing. Ask yourself things like: "Where was I? Who else was there? What was I wearing? Was I holding anything? What did I do?"

Don't be surprised if you are quite tired by now. You will only go into your visualization one more time. This time, intend to bring something back with you from that place and time to your present time and place. When you receive or see that item, come out of your trance and write down a description of what you brought back, again as specifically as possible.

Now, the interpretation. You have just gone to a place where you have had a past life. Even if the place you went felt like it was a current place (e.g. had cars or other modern-day indicators) the location was still a place, city, country, or location where you have lived in a past life.

The person or being that met you there is a person whom you knew in that past life and, more importantly, is also a person whom you know in this current lifetime. Or possibly it could be a person you have yet to meet in this lifetime.

The activity that you were doing has something to do with the reason you have returned to earth in this current lifetime. It is something you are still needing to do or finish.

Lastly, the thing you were given or that you took back from that lifetime symbolizes something (a personality trait, a challenge, a gift) that you have brought with you from that lifetime into this lifetime.

It will take quite some time to fully understand and interpret the meaning of your past-life visualization. You may even wish to do it again, returning to the same place so that you can notice and experience more details. This visualization may seem very real to you. Some people even smell fragrances or hear music or feel the clothes on their skin. In contrast, it may seem dreamlike or unreal. Either way is perfect, so don't judge what you learn by how you think it should have gone.

When you are done interpreting this exercise you should have a great deal of new information about yourself. You will have discovered four things:

1) A location or country where you have lived before in a past life.

2) A person who you know or will meet in this lifetime and have also known in a past life. Note: this person may look and be completely different now (i.e. different sex, age, etc.) but something about the person will be familiar and remind you of someone you know.

3) An occupation or mission you had in a past life that still has meaning in this one. It is likely something that you may need to do or finish in order to continue growing.

4) A gift, challenge, or trait you have brought with you from one life to the next. You might want to ponder why you brought it along and what you wish to do with it.

As an example, here is what I visualized when I did this exercise:

I went to a place I thought of as Persia (perhaps Turkey or Iran today). I had on what I can only describe as a belly dancing costume. I was met by a large man who seemed to be my handler or perhaps manager. I liked him, but did not totally trust him to have my best interests at heart. He took me to a large hall where I was forced to dance for a crowd of men. I wore beautiful silk veils which, as I danced, I gradually took off one by one. I felt safe in my veils but as each veil dropped I felt increasingly vulnerable. When I left the visualization I had only one veil on my body. I left the visualization at that time, bringing that one veil with me to this lifetime.

I laughed when I had this vision as the Middle East is a part of the world where I don't feel overly comfortable or safe. I debated who the man was in this lifetime, finally realizing he was/is a former agent of mine whom I like very much, but with whom I had some trust and other issues.

In my dance I felt very secretive, safe, and hidden until I released and let go of each veil. Every time I took off a veil I felt more and more vulnerable. My interpretation was that my past life contained elements of always keeping secrets from a crowd. I was in the room with the crowd but apart from it at the same time. I also had some trust issues in that lifetime. I believe I brought those issues into my current lifetime in order to work through them again. In this lifetime I am a psychic and also, in a way, a performer. I often work on a stage, giving talks and demonstrations. One tricky part of my current life is drawing the line between being too public or too solitary. In my visualization I only brought back one veil, though, so my interpretation is that I can stay only a little hidden in this lifetime. I do, though, have that veil to cover parts of myself that I am not willing to share or when I wish to keep secrets.

If you truly spend the time and effort that it takes on this exercise you will be rewarded with amazing insights into your personality, your mission, the people in your life, and much more. As with every intuitive experience, you will get as much out of past-life exercises and experiences as you are willing to spend on them.

chapter nine

*You've gotta dance like
there's nobody watching.*

—WILLIAM W. PURKEY

Dance like No One
Is Watching

If I didn't travel I would live a rather dull life. In my ordinary real life I tend to be fairly quiet and solitary. I read, write, work on my computer, and paint...not exactly high-adventure activities. There is something about traveling, though, that challenges me to be braver and take more chances, and do things I would never dream of doing if I were at home.

Because I was a sickly child, I never learned to be athletic or to take part in sports. I also have very little natural coordination. So, as an adult, it makes sense that my hobbies and activities and jobs have all been based on thinking and not on acting. For a long time I truly believed that I was simply incapable of playing sports or doing most physical activities. Travel though, by its very nature, demands that you move, often a lot. At minimum you need to be able to walk fairly long distances, climb stairs and hills, and haul around a suitcase containing everything you need for weeks at a time. It also presents many opportunities to do things that you simply would never have the chance or inclination to do at home.

Fear is a joy killer. It keeps you from doing things that you might very well enjoy and which are generally quite safe. As a child I was afraid of almost everything. I was also so self-conscious about my lack of ability that it was easier, I thought, not to even try rather than to risk making a fool of myself. A funny thing about traveling is that it has made me braver. When I travel I seem to no longer care what people think about me. After all, I am never going to see any of them again anyhow, so I can be whoever I want to be. After a while, I realized I was acting that way at home also. Travel changes you. Being a psychic wanderer is an act of courage.

When I was a teenager I had what I now realize was a gorgeous body but, at the time, I really believed I was too ugly to wear a bathing suit. I never really learned how to swim but I am a natural floater. So, when I finally dared to put on a bathing suit I learned two things: 1) no one really looks at me and 2) floating is all that is really important in the water.

I was leading a mystical trip to Mexico and the Mayan ruins many years ago and we were blessed to be allowed to do a type of sweat ceremony deep in the jungles of the Yucatan. I have done several Native American sweat ceremonies and this one was similar but also different, in that the lodge was much larger, had air holes with sunshine and fresh air coming in, and therefore was less hot. Still, we were all drenched in sweat by the time the ceremony was over after an hour or so.

We had all worn only a sarong into the ceremony and, when we were finished, none of us really wanted to put our soaked and dirty bodies back into our clothes. The Mayan people merely pointed to a cenote on the outskirts of their tiny village. The cenote was filled with fresh water and was open to the sky. It looked very refreshing.

Without really thinking I threw off my sarong and lowered myself into the cool clear water. (I really wanted to write that I dove in but truth won out. I have never dived into anything except life.) It wasn't until I was in the water that I remembered I was now naked and that the only way OUT of the water was to climb up a rope ladder in front of an entire Mayan village and all the participants of my trip. Then the most amazing thing happened. One by one almost everyone stripped and joined me until the cenote was filled with bobbing, joyful, free people playing and laughing. By the time we were ready to climb out, all of our self-doubts and self-consciousness had been cleansed away. It felt natural and freeing and is one of the things people still talk about many years later.

The wonderful thing is, the more that you do, the more you realize how much you are capable of doing. One of the many things that terrified me as a child were large animals. Even though I was raised on a farm, I did my very best to avoid the animals. Because I was allergic to almost everything, I didn't have to help with outdoor and barn chores and I chose to pretend the barn and the animals didn't exist. I am also somewhat of a clean freak and barns and animals simply are not overly clean (at least not the barn we had).

I think when you are afraid of things life tends to put those things into your path so that you can learn from them. At least that has happened to me with animals. I have ridden a horse once in my life and found it to be a terrifying experience. I didn't feel at all safe, nor did I feel the bonding some people tell me they feel with horses. All I felt was a strong desire to get off as soon as possible. After that, I decided riding animals was simply nothing I needed to do in my life.

So, of course, I am often presented with that challenge. In Egypt our group was taken to the Monastery of St. Simeon, which is surrounded by vast desert sands. This was the type of desert you see in the movies where, if you walk in the sand, you sink in over your ankles. The monastery was amazing but, when it was time to go, I learned that the only way out was by way of camel. There was NO way I was getting on such a tall and stinky creature. Unfortunately, my alternative was to walk through the burning sand, which they assured me I would be unable to do. So, ride I did. It wasn't pleasant or pretty but I did it and I arrived at our destination safely, if sore.

That is the way of psychic wandering. It not only opens up your third eye to seeing things in different ways, but it sometimes creates adventures that challenge your comfort zone. Usually, of course, you have a choice about doing something that is frightening for you. I have turned down riding an elephant on a number of occasions, being somewhat shocked that others really want to get on something that big and smelly. On the occasions when I have had to do something, though, I have found a pool of courage within me and been able to do things I would not have dreamed of doing before.

What are you afraid of?

It is useful to examine your fears on occasion to see if they really serve you. In this exercise all you need to do is sit quietly, loosen your tongue and relax, and then, with a piece of paper before you, list the things that make you fearful. After you have made your list, cross off all the fears that have been caused by something that happened to you in your lifetime. It should be easy for you to remember what brought them into being (for example, you fell off a roof when you were small and have ever since been afraid of heights).

The remaining items on the list are what you can concern yourself with in this exercise. Later, if you wish, you can also ask yourself if the other fears are still valid. For now, just focus on the fears you seem to have been born having. These, in my opinion, are often rooted in another lifetime or perhaps are fears that belong to someone else (e.g. your mother was afraid of dogs so you are as well).

For the purpose of this exercise it is not necessary to know when these fears originated or why you have these fears. Remember that when and why questions really don't help us much. What you need to ask are two questions:

1) Do I wish to continue to have this fear? If the answer is no, then ask:

2) What can I do to challenge myself to face the fear?

As the stories above illustrate, I have learned that the universe tends to put you in situations where you are forced to meet and face your fears. It is easier, though, if we create these situations and put our own souls in control, rather than letting the cosmos push us. To do that, you might want to gently ease your way into doing what you fear. If you are afraid of public speaking, perhaps volunteer to give the announcements at a meeting. If you are fearful in crowds, go to an event that you will enjoy and let yourself mingle with the crowd for a bit. Make a commitment to yourself to very gently push yourself to face a fear or two. You can take baby steps, especially at home. Traveling is apt to push you a bit harder. Being a psychic wanderer will stretch your limits, so preparing a bit at home is a good practice.

Everyone's comfort zone is completely different. I have no fear of heights, so I have eagerly flown in hot air balloons in Egypt and Kenya, in a helicopter in New Zealand and an open barn-stormer plane in Sedona, Arizona, but when I was presented with the opportunity to take a zip-line in Guatemala, my fear came forward once again.

The fear, I realized, was because I am mechanically challenged. A zip-line is a very simple piece of machinery, consisting of a pulley suspended on a cable. You are then strapped onto this pulley and pushed off a decline. The zip-line course in Guatemala was a series of ten cables winding themselves down a mountain. You climbed to the top and zipped down to the bottom. The climb didn't bother me, nor did the fact that the cables were hundreds of feet above the ground. I wasn't even too concerned that the workers all smelled like they had had beer for breakfast. What scared me was that I was given a heavy leather glove and told that in order to stop I had to use the glove to brake with my hand. I was certain I would lose the glove, forget to brake and slam into the mountain, or brake too soon and hang suspended in the middle.

Sometimes you have to face your fear and do it anyhow. Other times though, life gives you guardian angels to help you. My guardian angel on this ride was a young Guatemalan man who offered to be strapped behind me and do my braking. He had obviously been partying with the others that morning but I gratefully accepted the assistance and enjoyed the ride without worrying about how I would stop.

I realized that there would have been a time in my life when I would have been embarrassed to zip-line down a slope with a Guatemalan strapped to my back (real women brake for themselves!), but that time had long passed. Travel had changed me from the girl who was too self-conscious to appear in a bathing suit to the woman who laughed at how silly she must look with a man strapped to her rear.

The authors and husbands laugh like no one is watching.

It is absolutely amazing how freeing it is to no longer care what you look like. The old adage, "Dance as if no one is watching," is wonderful advice. Because the truth is, no one

IS watching or, at least, no one cares. Most people are far too busy worrying about themselves to pay much attention to us.

Even when someone is watching, it really doesn't matter much either. I learned this many years ago in Belo Horizonte, Brazil. My husband had connected with two Brazilian couples at a Lion's International convention in Minneapolis. They had come for the convention and had stayed with us for a week or so. We became fast friends and a year later we went to Brazil to visit them. It was a surprise to see our friends in their home environment. The couple with whom we stayed were, as it turned out, quite wealthy, and we were richly entertained and spoiled by them. One night they decided we needed to experience a Brazilian dance club and took us to their favorite one.

We had not packed to go out on the town. When I travel I dress very simply, generally in jeans and shirts and sensible shoes. I luckily had brought a skirt along but that was as much finery as my wardrobe allowed.

Our hosts, Silvio and Carmina, are elegant people and are well-known and respected in Brazilian society. We were ushered to the best front-row table. All the women were dressed in magnificent dancing gowns and some of them even changed their outfits several times during the night. I felt like a thorn in a bed of roses, but comforted myself with the anonymity of sitting at a darkened table and watching as the dancers created a spectacular Samba show. Then, the lights came up and we were introduced to the crowd.

Apparently, visitors from out of the country are expected to dance. My husband, Loren, flatly refused. He has two left feet and would no more dance in front of a crowd than he would fly to the moon. For some reason, though, that did not let me off the hook. Nor did saying that I didn't know how to dance the Samba.

A handsome, dashing young man appeared who promised me that he could teach me to Samba. He was the club's dance instructor and assured me that "anyone as lovely as me could learn it easily." Of course, this was translated to me from his Portuguese so what he may really have said is: "You have GOT to be kidding!"

I had no choice but to go out on the floor in my sensible tourist outfit and start to dance with my dashing instructor. Then, like something out of a nightmare, a spotlight was turned on us and everyone else left the floor to watch our dance.

After a moment of sheer panic I realized there was really no choice but to relax and enjoy it. The instructor was amazingly talented and once I simply relaxed and followed his lead, I found myself having a marvelous time. The dance ended, people clapped and thankfully other dancers returned to the floor. I was escorted back to our table, shaken but triumphant.

What I realized from that experience is that when you have no choice, you can not only do things you would never dream of, but you can actually enjoy doing them. I can think of no other circumstances under which I would dance in front of a crowd. I not only did it though, I enjoyed it. As far as I know, no one laughed (at least out loud) and no one really noticed or cared how I was dressed.

A similar thing happened to me in Mexico where we were visiting Xcaret, a natural aquarium park near Cancun. I was excited to see that they offered dolphin swims, something I had always wanted to experience. Unfortunately, and rather typically of me, I did not get the full information about the swim before I signed up and paid for it.

I had a lovely fantasy of getting into the water with gentle creatures and swimming alongside them in the open sea. Instead, I was ushered into a small lagoon where six dolphins were confined and sentenced to a lifetime of playing with tourists. Worse, there were stadium seats set up on either side of the lagoon with an audience watching the performance while the trainer narrated the event. Instead of the quiet swim I had anticipated, I had become part of a forced animal show.

The other thing I had not anticipated is that dolphins are BIG and scary. Once in the water I was committed, gritting my teeth as dolphins pushed me through the water by the soles of my feet (NOT a pretty sight!) and jumped over a line of us from behind. It felt as though both the dolphins and the people had been trapped in the lagoon and forced to perform. The difference, of course, is that I got to leave when it was over.

As this was happening, I realized I could hate every moment of it or I could find the beauty of the experience. For there was beauty and majesty being in the water with such magnificent creatures. To find the shred of joy in those moments I had to let go of a lot. I had to release my judgment, at least for a moment, of how wrong it was to confine dolphins and force them to perform. I had to let go of my self-consciousness at having one hundred people watch me in an unflattering bathing suit being pushed headlong across a lagoon by my feet. I also had to forget I had paid a fair amount of money for that humiliation.

There were moments when the dolphin came near to me, nudging me, almost seeming to comfort and encourage the poor woman who was both embarrassed and ashamed to be there. Then I realized that, while I would never do that again, it would not help the dolphin or me to hate the experience. So, to the best that I could, I found the joy in being with such a magnificent creature. I could wait until I got home to lobby for that sort of practice to be banned.

The strange thing about fear is that what we fear is so individualized. It is hard, sometimes, to understand another person's fears unless we happen to share them. To some people, as Jean describes below, America can be a frightening place full of terrifying uncertainty. For most of us, it is simply home.

> *A large part of travel for me is learning to trust the universe and to overcome my fears. Each time I step onto a plane I am allowing myself to give my well-being over to another, to accept that I am not in charge of this world. Of course, it is just an illusion to think we are in control of our lives at any moment ... but it is crystal clear when we travel.*
>
> *Fear can limit us so. This became very clear to me when our relatives from the Netherlands were planning their visit. They were well traveled in the EU, but had never been to this continent. Countless emails were exchanged about whether they could drink our water, whether it was safe to carry cash, and could they access safe medications if they needed them? They finally decided against visiting New York and Florida because all the travel message boards on the Dutch internet said that crime was too high and it was too dangerous for foreigners.*
>
> *Their perception of America was one of danger and loaded hand guns, a gang member on every street corner in*

each city, and religious zealots and serial murderers lurking in every small town.

Our cousins are educated and thoughtful people. If they truly stopped and reflected they would acknowledge that they knew these stereotypes were false. But their fear did stop them from seeing some of the major sites they wanted to visit, and I do not think they would have dared to come to exotic America without us here to buffer and encourage.

Of course, it is a LOT easier to laugh at fear when it is someone else's. I have always found Jean's fear of bats to be a bit silly. After all, they are not truly scary … like spiders and snakes. No matter what our fear is, though, it is very real to us. Travel seems to bring these fears to the surface and then help us to realize that we are capable of "feeling the fear and doing it anyhow." As Jean tells it:

Perhaps because of a chaotic childhood or the inherent challenges of being intuitive; perhaps I was just born this way, but I love the illusion of stability and I hate change. I am a born nester and seek out routine. So it was very difficult for me to realize in my thirties that I needed to step outside of my comfort zones to continue growing as a human being. I was becoming complacent and rigid, two of the traits I despise in others.

Travel allows me to really challenge myself in dramatic ways and learn more about myself in just a few minutes than I would in years at home. Because I enjoy more adventuresome travel, I have had to face down my fears time after time. I am proud of the changes I have made and fears I have faced.

Carl Jung stated, "What you resist not only persists, but will grow in size." It is in essence the Law of Attraction; one tends to attract that which one fears most. I have had numerous and terrifying home invasions by bats. I am absolutely phobic about them, and once left an apartment I had rented due to an infestation of them in the attic. I left at midnight one night and never returned. My friends and family had to pack up my belongings and move me.

Years later, my husband, his sister Mary, and I sat in a beach café watching the sun set over the Indian ocean. A perfect setting, waiting for our perfect Balinese dinner to arrive. Tranquil, peaceful … terrifying? Bats the size of small eagles were flitting in and out of the café. I was instantly sick to my stomach and ready to leave. Instead, I wore my menu as a hat for the entire meal and forced myself to stay. I have rarely been as proud of myself.

It did not cure my phobia, of course, but once I had looked a fruit bat with a three-foot wingspan in the eyes, I was well on my way.

Six years later my darling husband convinced me to go by dugout canoe up a river in the Costa Rica mountains. We passed over the unmarked border into Panama on the other side of the river, boarded an old bus that broke down twice, and landed in a very small village. There we were escorted to a ritual that had been arranged with the local Shaman.

As four of us waited to enter the palm hut, we were told by the English-speaking villager that it was very important that we take off our hats and that we must remain silent during the ceremony. Once we entered we could not leave the ceremony. In we filed and our group of four sat on the ground in front of the elderly man. He began to chant and burn incense, which was lovely until the bats that nested in the thatching reacted.

This small building was suddenly filled with several swooping bats. I could not cover my head, leave, or scream. I did grab my husband's leg for protection, and he ended up with a lovely imprint of my finger tips for a bruise.

Again, I somehow survived. I reached inside myself to a place where tranquility dwelled, and made it through the ceremony.

I can now even go into caves and old temples and enjoy the experience (but still not the bats), and better yet....I can sit outside in Minnesota at night and tolerate the bats that fly at dusk.

Both Jean and I suffer from claustrophobia to a certain extent. I have vague past-life memories of being buried alive (a memory I do NOT wish to allow to surface) and so for years, even getting into an elevator was a challenge for me. Claustrophobia is debilitating in many ways and so, as I suggest you do in the above exercise, I forced myself to take baby steps to face it. I started with elevators, as they are a necessary thing in our modern life. After I was able to ride in one without pure panic, I could move on to airplanes and, the more I entered into small spaces and survived, the calmer I became. It also helps to realize, on a conscious level at least, that it is highly unlikely that I will be buried alive in this lifetime. So, once you have your lists of fears, take baby steps to face them. Your life will improve.

Here, Jean tells about facing her own claustrophobia while wandering:

After we booked our family vacation to Turkey I immediately began to fret about a tour we were taking to the underground cities of Cappadocia. I am claustrophobic, and in order to see the underground cities I had to go several stories underground, crouching through the tunnels that connected the rooms.

I was worried for months, arguing with myself and giving myself permission to skip the tour. That morning I simply decided to do it, trusting in spirit to support me and give me the strength I needed.

What a wonderful experience, seeing where the ancient Christians and Crusaders had lived for years underground to escape persecution (and there were no bats!). Knowing I could face down a fear I had simply accepted in myself for decades and conquer it was priceless and life changing.

In New Zealand Kathryn and I, with our spouses, booked a helicopter tour of the glacier areas and mountains. I was so excited about it, thrilled that I was going to have this once-in-a-lifetime experience. I even dreamed about it in advance, how beautiful it was going to be.

As we lifted off the mountaintop I almost jumped out of the helicopter…I hated every minute of the hour we spent in the air. It was so windy, the control tower immediately grounded all flights for the remainder of the day, and ordered all aircraft back to the base. We landed on a mountain glacier for photographs, and it took the pilot and my three companions to get me back in that machine to return to the landing strip.

I am very glad I did it and very glad I do not need to do it again.

The world can shrink down to a very small, very boring place if we do not stretch and challenge ourselves. It is far too easy to define ourselves by our limitations and comfort levels rather than finding the depth and strength and joy that we contain.

My mother-in-law, Gladys Blume, is a constant inspiration to me. She shows me daily what it means to age with grace and wit. When she heard that we were going to India she shocked me by asking if she could come along as she had never shown any interest in any other destination to which we had traveled. Although she was 66 years old, had just had two knee replacements, and knew her mobility might be compromised, she packed her bags and made her childhood dream journey come true.

With assistance from her daughter, Mary, and my husband, Fred, she completed a sixteen-day trip that left many younger travelers exhausted. She braved temperatures over 110 degrees, poor food, and challengingly long days on a bus without complaint. She had decided what was important to her, and used her limited energy to make sure she experienced those things.

She rode an elephant to the Red Fort in Jaipur, placed a rock on Gandhi's grave and rode a jeep into the Indian jungle at night. She saw a lot of India from the window of a bus, and if she couldn't walk through a site she would happily sit outside the bus with Mr. Singh, our Sikh bus driver. They had many interesting discussions, and we were shocked one day when Gladys disclosed that Mr. Singh had removed his turban and unwound his hair to show her its length. (Sikhs do not cut their hair as part of their religious observance).

While we were off exploring the external world, Gladys found friends and adventures in the microcosm of India she COULD experience. She always had a new story of an acquaintance made, tea offered to her by a local woman who saw her sitting on a bench, an animal or bird only she saw. We soon went from feeling sorry that she could not walk the streets of Delhi to envying her the slow and thoughtful understanding she was forming of such a complex country.

She embodied bravery and humor for me that trip, but the sweetest moment was when she saw her husband of forty years at the airport at home! They ran toward each other with tears in their eyes and, may I say, we had tears in ours. They had never been apart for so long. Still, even her deep love for him did not stand in the way of her fearlessly following her heart.

For at least the brief period of my adventure travels I want to be fearless, I want to take the helicopter ride over the New Zealand glacier, zip-line over a rainforest canopy and snorkel on the reef. So that means taking rational risks and a leap of faith, facing my fears and grabbing the moment. Then, again, so does living any life worth living.

Travel strips away the pretensions we all carry with us in our day-to-day lives. We wear the same clothes for days on end, our makeup goes unused, our hair is tucked under a hat, and, as a tourist, you get away with not knowing how to do things. You can be silly and have fun and even be a tad reckless. It is almost like getting to be a kid again.

As psychic wanderers, we can carry these attitudes home with us. We can be just as brave in the pool at the Y or our nephew's wedding dance. We can eat new foods at home as much as we can when we travel. We can finally realize that most people are so busy watching themselves that they have no time at all to think about us.

Being a psychic wanderer teaches you a type of courage that will stand you in good stead in your life as an intuitive. After all, anyone claiming to be psychic is immediately branded as a fraud, or at least a nutcase, by many if not most people. To be a master intuitive we must be able to not care what people think about us. We need to have the courage to act upon our intuitive knowings without always being able to explain our behavior. We need to be brave enough to dance like no one is watching…even when they are.

chapter ten

Speak to the earth,
and it will teach you.
—THE BIBLE, JOB 12:7-10

When Rocks Talk

Someone asked me, not too long ago, what the difference was between spiritual travel and "regular" travel. It is a very good question because all travel can and usually does have a spiritual component. Who has not stood in awe and wonder at a site of natural splendor? Who hasn't thanked the universe, God, or whatever you may call the divine, for the beauty of the world? Travel, particularly in nature, has a way of making the divine come alive in our souls.

Psychic wandering, though, goes beyond spontaneous moments of communion with the divine to intentionally seeking out those moments. I suppose, to answer my friend's question in a nutshell, the difference between ordinary and spiritual travel is that mystical travelers pay attention to the energy of each place, purposely seeking information and guidance.

Everything in the universe has a type of energy (and yes, I know that term is over-used and under-defined, but it is the best I have) that we can feel, read, and even sometimes see with our physical eyes. We have talked about reading the energy of other people and how valuable it is to do when traveling. Sensing and feeling the energy of places and things is just as worthwhile and will give a psychic wanderer an enormous amount of insight and awareness, not only of the place but also of his- or herself.

In psychic parlance, the word for reading the energy of objects is psychometry. Many of you use psychometry all the time, although you may never have had a name for it before. Psychometry is simply reading the energy of, and picking up information from, material objects. Many of us use it every time we go shopping. You may have had the experience of seeing something in a store and loving it until you picked it up. Then, after touching it, realizing it wasn't for you. You may find that you need to handle all the vitamin bottles, for example, before you can choose the brand that is right for you. Retailers have learned that people like to handle things before they buy them. They have discovered that things placed at the level of our hands tend to sell quickest. It is one of the things I miss when shopping online or through catalogs. I like to read the vibrations of an object before I bring it into my house.

All things have a natural vibration or aura. We are well aware of that in our human bodies, but most have a more difficult time believing that rocks or soil (or socks!) also vibrate. Scientists, while they certainly would not agree with most of my premises, will tell you that the earth and everything on it vibrates in some way. Part of what psychic wandering is all about is taking the time to feel and listen to these vibrations and then to ask for and receive information from these things.

The beauty of traveling is that we can take the time to really feel a place and its objects. It just seems natural to touch things when we travel. Even less metaphysically minded tourists want to touch rocks and statues and buildings. I always feel a bit sad at the sites that ask us not to touch things, although I know it is for the good purpose of protecting the antiquities. I never feel that I quite know something unless I am able to physically touch it. It is true for me about touching people as well. I think it is why I first gravitated to reading palms. It was a sneaky way of being able to hold a person's hand and read their soul.

Jean tells about her experience with a simple stone column in Turkey.

In Ephesus I had the strongest psychometric experience I have ever had. I merely brushed against a pillar outside of a merchant's house. The energy pulsed up my arm and I tingled all the way to my head. My arm turned a bright red and remained that way for an hour. Kathryn also touched it and felt a great deal of energy, but nowhere near the electric shock I had experienced.

Here is the mystery of travel. Certainly, one can understand feeling the resonance of the violence and cheering when touching a seat in the stadium in Perge where more than fifteen thousand spectators cheered on the lions against the Christians. Why, though, would a nondescript

pillar outside of an unimportant shopkeeper's house hold
so much energy? I will never know, but it was a fascinating
experience that I still ponder. How much of our initial reac-
tion to places is based on energy we do not fully understand?

Along with the natural vibration of all matter, objects pick up pieces of the vibrations or energy field of the person or persons who have been in contact with them. This is one explanation for why ancient sites contain such a huge amount of energy. Imagine how many people have walked through the Colosseum, for example. For those of us who pay attention, the very stones and building material of a place hold pieces of the stories of each person who has had contact with it.

Ancient rocks and trees in Angkor Wat.

Leave only positive energy

Many of these stories are tragic, which explains how grief can sometimes spontaneously bubble up inside us at ancient and not-so-ancient sites. Always remember to ask "Is this mine?" when you feel an inexplicable emotion come upon you for no reason. We can pick up vibrations and emotions of places and things without being consciously aware of them and, unless we identify the source, we can carry them around for longer than we need. Also remember that you, too, are leaving your vibrational mark on each site. The slogan, "Take only photos, leave only footprints" should be amended to "leave only positive energy." Some of us are amazingly sloppy and litter our emotions all over the place.

I believe that some sites are more energetically porous than others and pick up our emotional energy more easily. If the energy left there is loving and gentle, these sites become wonderful places to meditate and linger. In other sites, though, I often feel a strong desire to leave quickly because of the fear and grief that linger in the ground itself.

Many years ago my husband and I visited the site of the concentration camp at Dachau, Germany. I had not expected, of course, that it would be an upbeat visit, but I was not prepared for the very ground to still be sobbing. As if in sympathy, the skies opened and a cold rain poured on us as we toured the site. It stopped the minute we drove away.

It is estimated that over two hundred thousand prisoners were housed there during the Second World War and that at least twenty-five thousand of these were killed or died of malnutrition or disease. Seeing the exhibits, dormitories, even the gas chamber were chilling enough, but the vibrations from all the fear and pain were close to being overwhelming for us both.

I felt the same way at the Holocaust Museum in Washington, DC. There the building was new and the ground had not been walked upon by such horror, yet the objects that were housed there still carried these strong vibrations. My experience is that most museums have a great deal of emotional leakage. It is one reason that, though I love them, I also can only stay an hour or so before needing to get into fresh air and sunshine.

Whenever you travel to a place where many people are or have been, remember to do the cleansing and protection exercises we have given you. I find hospitals, airports, shopping malls, fairs, and events to be exhausting emotionally and psychically.

Like sites, some objects seem to pick up energy more easily than others. Crystals and metallic jewelry seem to be particularly sensitive to energy vibrations. That is why most intuition trainers use jewelry or other objects worn or handled frequently as good items with which to begin teaching psychometry. After you have learned the technique, though, you can get information from paper, leather, wood, clothing, and virtually any other material object.

How to do Psychometry

Sometimes, you want to be able to read an object. Often when I am traveling I get good intuitive information just from bending down to pick up a rock from the ground and holding it for a few minutes. If you want to get information from a particular item, start by putting yourself into a relaxed, focused state, then ask yourself what you feel, hear, think, or see in your mind's eye. If possible, hold the item while focusing and notice what emotional feelings you have, what you see in your mind's eye, or what thoughts come to mind. If you feel that you are not getting anything, remind yourself that it is impossible to sit long without a thought, and use whatever thought appears in your mind.

After you get a hit from the item (whether it is an emotion, mind picture, thought, perhaps a physical reaction, or a combination of these) you can then interpret it. You don't need it to be an elaborate process or message. Good questions to ask are things like, "What does this emotion or picture or thought mean to me?" or "What message did this thing have for me?" I think you will be surprised at how helpful your answers will be to you ... and how fun!

You can do this at home as well, of course. Ask the objects with which you come in contact to speak to you. You don't need to let anyone know you are doing this if you don't want to—you can just let them wonder why life is seeming to go better for you lately.

Using this technique is extremely helpful during your souvenir shopping or any type of shopping for that matter. Most travelers love to buy things when on vacation. I am no exception. My house is a museum, of sorts, full of statues, paintings, and other items I have bought around the world. Always remember, though, that everything carries a vibration that you are bringing into your home.

Jean's and my parents loved antiques and junk and often didn't differentiate between the two. Our childhood home was a mishmash of lovely old furniture and not-so-lovely (to my eye) knickknacks. As a young adult, more out of poorness than choice, my own home was furnished with hand-me-downs and garage sale goods. As I grew older and had more money I was able to buy better furniture, but I still loved going to garage sales and antique and junk stores. Now though, I find I can barely stand going into them. The items all chatter at me, telling me their tales.

The more you have handled an item and the stronger the emotions experienced while wearing or using an item, the more an item will speak to you. This can be lovely. Old bibles, bridal dresses, cribs, and kitchen appliances often have a sweet, beautiful, loving energy. Other items, though, if used in anger or simply during sad times, might have a melancholy vibration.

Questions to ask before purchasing an item

Because of this, it is important, whether you are buying a souvenir at the Grand Bazaar in Istanbul or a used table at Goodwill, to ask: "How does this item make me feel?" "What mental pictures come to mind when I handle it?" "How will its vibrations match with the energy of my home?" Far too many purchases are never used or are simply not liked once they get home. Often it is because the person didn't ask the item to tell about itself.

After a visit to the Terra Cotta Army in Xian, China, visitors are ushered into a huge gift store containing hundreds of replicas of the real thing. The Terra Cotta Army is a collection of terra cotta sculptures depicting the armies of Qin Shi Huang, the first Emperor of China. It is a form of funerary art buried with the emperor in 210–209 BC. It is said that the purpose of the army was to protect the emperor in his afterlife, and to make sure that he had people to rule over. Over eight thousand life-size terra cotta soldiers, horses, and other figures were buried along with the Emperor. They were discovered in 1974 by a group of farmers digging a well. Nowadays they are a major tourist attraction and huge income-generating site.

Truth be told, I didn't like the terra cotta soldiers (either the real ones OR the replicas). The sight of all those life-size warriors, still buried in pits, was amazing and certainly worth seeing, but the entire exhibit gave me the chills. In addition to glorifying war, it seemed dark and gloomy and sad to me. So, why did I turn around and buy four small statues to take home with me? I suppose, like many tourists, just because I was there and wanted a memento of my visit.

When I got the small statues home I couldn't find a place that felt right for them. All the other statues I had bought around the world were proudly displayed, but the soldiers just felt wrong wherever I placed them. Still, I kept them. After all, I had bought them and they were memories of a good trip.

Almost immediately, though the figures began to break. One was knocked over by a guest, another shattered by my cleaning lady, one of them actually seemed to lose an arm all on his own. Each time one broke I felt a tiny bit of relief. They carried an energy that simply was not compatible with mine.

To prove I don't always do as I say, the last remaining statue still remains in my husband's office, refusing to break. I think it is because Loren likes it.

In contrast, I bought a ceremonial mask in Kenya that is quite frightening to look at. The mask has a fierce, warrior-like expression and carries with it the energy of many people who have handled it over a hundred years or so. Despite that, it feels perfectly at home next to a serene Buddha statue. Every time I look at it I feel a flush of power and a wild and glorious urge to run free. It was the perfect souvenir of a land that also made me feel that way.

The very act of purchasing something can change you in some way. Then, each time you look at it or handle it, your intuition reminds you of why it is important. It acts, in a way, like a totem or visual reminder of your psychic message.

Here, Jean tells about a statue she bought in Turkey and what it means to her:

As I write this I am looking at a six-inch bust of Medusa (a statue of a Greek Gorgon, a female whose hair consists of snake heads—she embodied female power and strength), hand-carved from raw turquoise and very unique. It remains one of my favorite mementoes, and I often pick it up and let it transport me back in time. Our family had just toured Ephesus and we were returning to the van through a row of aggressive shop owners. Rejecting the sameness of the wares in most of the shops, we turned off to the side row and saw our first woman shop owner. (Turkey, while a liberal Muslim country, is still very much male dominated.) She had beautiful, but expensive, items for sale.

I immediately spotted my Medusa. I am terrible; if there is haggling involved, I usually just leave, so Kathryn stepped in to bargain for me. After getting the price down to where I did not feel TOO guilty, the shopkeeper was bundling it up for me as she spoke.

"It is made by the only woman in Turkey who carves stone," said the older woman. As we left she asked us, "Are you sisters?" and then asked if she could kiss me. I was kissed on both cheeks; Kathryn was blessed with kisses also. She then smiled and said, "I am so happy this statue goes home with women."

I am so glad to have the statue, not only because it is beautiful but because I am reminded that the sisterhood of women crosses all nationalities and borders. One purchase at a time I can make a difference.

The joy of Beachcombing

Some of my very favorite souvenirs don't cost a penny. If I had to choose one pastime over all others, I think it would be beachcombing. I have an ability to walk down a beach, gazing at nothing, looking everywhere and waiting for the perfect item to call my name. I can walk for hours, filling my pockets with what I call pretties. These shiny stones, sea shells, fragments of long-ago broken bottles, and other items all call out asking to be talked to, admired, and examined. Into my pockets they go.

Later, usually in the shade with a cold drink, I ask each one if it wishes to go home with me. Luckily, generally only one or two of them do. The rest are brought back to the beach to converse with and be found by others. Over the years I have accumulated enough small rocks and shells to fill many a dish in my house and yard. I love how their energy feels when they are all mixed together, like a little United Nations of stones and trinkets sitting on a coffee table.

Jean's husband, Fred, loves rocks the way I love sea shells. Here is how they have solved the "too many rocks" dilemma.

My husband, Fred, loves rocks. His mother says from the time he could crawl she was removing pebbles from his tightly clenched fist and checking pockets before washing his jeans. He has, literally, never met a rock he did not love. Even if the rock is not beautiful or gemlike, it has character and a story in his eyes.

As lovely as this joyful hobby is for him, it presents major issues for us as travelers. There are just a limited number of pounds of rocks one can carry home. We actually shipped fifty pounds of rocks home from California one time, only to find that the post office had quarantined them because of the smell (they were taken right off the beach). Apparently, sitting in a sealed box in a hot truck does not improve the ocean's odor.

It was only after numerous arguments and countless over-weight baggage charges that we finally reached a compromise. I would stop nagging him about all the rocks he was picking up, and he would promise to only bring home a few.

Now, the evening before we board any aircraft home is filled with the ritual of "catch and release." We take an hour or so, often joined by other travelers, to sort through Fred's cache and decide which few rocks have actual value and meaning to us. Often we will cradle a rock in our hands and take the time to feel what it says to us. It is very inter-esting to find that stones can emanate the feelings of the site or country; they seem to hold the essence of the land within them and can transport us back to the place and time where we found them.

It is a wonderful opportunity to see that the joy is in the experience of finding the rock, memento, or shell … not in the actual object. We take a few minutes to relive the trip by reviewing the rocks, choosing a few, and releasing the others. I have also been able to release my tension over his rock gathering during the trip, knowing that we will find the perfect one or two to grace our home.

chapter eleven

If you don't like their rules,
whose would you use?

—CHARLIE BROWN

Rules for the Road

I am not a person who likes rules, unless I happen to make them. However, when traveling wherever you may go on life's journeys there are certain pointers that make the trip easier and more joyful.

Over the years, I have accumulated a number of rules (suggestions, really) that I tell the adventurers who join me in my journeys. As I thought about them, I also realized that they apply to our everyday lives as well.

I have led hundreds of spiritual and metaphysical seekers on journeys of all kinds. Some of the rules I advise them about are as follows:

1) Eat when you can, drink when you can, pee when you can.

In our day-to-day lives we become very complacent about things like bathrooms and food. Most, if not all, of the people reading this book have ready access to toilets and refrigerators. We are able to say, "I'll grab some food later" without concern that there may be no food later. We know that we can wait until it is necessary to use a toilet.

On the road though, these everyday and unthought-about functions become much more important. Meals are often delayed; clean or even close to clean public toilets are a rarity in some countries and are sometimes only a hole in the ground; the beverages that are available will not necessarily be your favorite brand. Ice, and even chilled drinks, is often available only at the finest hotels and restaurants. As it always does, traveling makes you much more aware of what you need and want and how it is not always just there for the taking. So, my advice to all travelers is to eat something whenever it is available (or at least take it along for later), drink water before you get thirsty, and to pee even if it isn't really necessary. I call it preemptive peeing. This prevents us from stopping along the road and searching for bushes.

The cosmic truth behind this rule is that life is not always predictable and controllable. Humans seem to crave a constancy in our lives to the extent that we almost believe in it. Traveling shakes up this belief. We suddenly discover that the most taken-for-granted things like clean water and clean toilets are not always available. We also discover we are far more resourceful than we thought. Women find out they can pee standing up, we discover we can eat foods we thought we were allergic to or drink a different brand of soda than we always order.

Once we realize that life isn't always as we expect it to be, the wise thing to do is to prepare for the unexpected. On the road, we learn to plan for restaurants being closed, mechanical issues, weather delays, and toilets so filthy we just can't go into them.

In our everyday lives, expecting the unexpected is also a good plan. We are entering an era of unprecedented change. During the next few years, many of the things we have relied upon (jobs, retirement accounts, family support, health insurance) may very well disappear. This is not meant to scare you, it is simply the way life on earth works. As in traveling, the wise person prepares for the worst and hopes for the best. Most importantly of all, she enjoys the journey no matter what happens, knowing she has the tools to cope with it.

2) Never stand when you can sit, walk when you can ride, or be in the sun if shade is available.

This rule takes people a bit of time to understand. After all, isn't it GOOD to walk? Doesn't the sun feel nice on a cool day? From years of experience, I can say, "Yes, it does, but you will likely do all the walking you can take by the end of the day and you may get more sun than your skin can handle."

This is, perhaps, a corollary to rule number one. Traveling often requires you to walk for longer and on rougher terrain than you expected. Once you are on a path, there is often no turning back until the end. You may have to stand in blistering sun to listen to a tour guide or because the site has no shade. So, when you have a choice, the smart traveler will choose comfort, knowing that comfort may not be available at the next stop.

On every trip I have ever led, at least one person seems intent on refusing to be comfortable. He or she feels a need to climb everything, walk everywhere, and stand, hatless, in the midday sun. Well, at least until the next day when he is sunburned and limping.

One life lesson I had to learn is that while pain may be inevitable, suffering is optional. I suppose I could list that as an optional excursion in my travel brochures. Many of us were raised to think that there is a certain honor in self-sacrifice. However, in life as in traveling, no one gives medals out just because you suffered to get there. Machu Picchu looks the same to those who arrive by train as it does to those who hiked the Inca trail. Sleeping in five-star hotels does not make your trip less worthy than sleeping in a hostel. It just gets you a better night's sleep.

I am not saying that there is no great value in hiking and taking the time to savor each step to a destination. I am in awe of people who climb Mount Everest, hike the Camino de Santiago in Spain, or crawl on their knees at the shrine of our Lady of Fatima. These types of journeys are perfect ways to challenge yourself, find self-knowledge, and take precious time to contemplate life. I am not so in awe of people who feel superior in their journeys because they have suffered to get there.

I have a fantasy of us all lined up, waiting to choose our life's path before we take the plunge and come to earth. Our guides show us a long list of things we can choose to experience, learn, and do. "Do you want wealth? Adventure? Do you want to mend a relationship or end one? What challenges do you want to learn to overcome? How about just taking it easy in this life? Maybe learn your lessons with less effort and have ample resources to enjoy life?" In my fantasy I always laugh, imagining so many saying, "Oh, no, I just couldn't take ease and comfort and joy. Give those to someone else. I'll just take whatever is left."

As we travel through life as well as through the world the wise person realizes the journey goes easier, both for us and for our companions, when we are rested, healthy, and comfortable. Our suffering helps no one and instead slows the group down.

3) Never bring anything you can't afford to lose.

This is a rule you hear a lot in many travel guides. Despite that, I am often amazed at the valuable things people carry when traveling. I once listened to the mourning of a man who had lost a five-hundred-dollar cigar lighter. I hate to admit it, but my sympathy was limited by the wonder of WHO would bring along such a lighter on a trip.

For psychic wanderers, however, the risk is not so much about having something lost or stolen as it is about the emotional and psychic effect its loss might have on you. It is also about how energetically burdened you may be by the items you bring. Everything we own also owns a bit of us. Sometimes ownership can be a burden. You have to store it, care for it, or repair it, insure it, decide when to get rid of it and how; and, when you are traveling, lug it around with you. Ownership can also be a joy. The item can remind you of happy times, serve you well by doing a necessary function, or simply be so beautiful it makes your soul sing. Still, whether burden or joy, each thing you own has an emotional and energetic attachment to you. The more you use or handle it, the larger this energy attachment becomes.

Packing for a journey, then, should not be just a quick toss a few things in a bag sort of experience. Everything you bring will either enhance or detract from your travels. Excess baggage, whether it is in your suitcase or emotional stuff you still carry around, will slow you down and burden you. I always think about that while lugging an overpacked suitcase through an airport or up a flight of hotel stairs.

Being mindful (the art of maintaining a calm awareness of your bodily functions, feelings, thoughts, and perceptions) is so much easier to do as a traveler than it is at home. This is because you are out of your ordinary surroundings and way of life and are thus more naturally open and aware. So, why not start this awareness and mindfulness when you start packing your suitcase?

You can find many packing guides on the Internet and in travel guides. Usually the most important piece of advice is left out. *Take what you need to enhance your journey. Leave behind anything that will detract from it.* What items are taken will vary widely from person to person. You may need to pack a few photos or symbols of something or someone you love, or a favorite book you read in the evening. Perhaps a few candles will remind you of home or maybe you simply can't sleep without your favorite pillow.

I often struggle with hotel pillows. I can adapt rather quickly to hard beds, cold rooms, or even noisy plumbing, but more nights than I care to admit have been spent tossing and fighting with a too-big pillow. As I was writing this chapter I realized that, perhaps, I need to bring my own pillow. I also am aware that some part of me feels too proud to be a person who lugs a pillow around with them. A wiser part of me knows that pride is a foolish reason to be uncomfortable. So, I have written "find a comfortable travel pillow" on my to-do list.

Before you leave on any journey, think of the things that are important for you to be able to sleep well and be comfortable on a journey. It might mean bringing ear plugs or air freshener or a good moisturizer. A portable sound machine is a good investment if it gives you good sleep.

This also means that you should bring clothing that makes you feel energetic, curious, and alive. Once, one of my fellow travelers decided to pack only old, worn-out, and disliked clothes, wear them, and then leave them behind, filling her empty suitcase with souvenirs. When she first mentioned it, it seemed to be a great idea. Everyone liked the idea of leaving clothes behind in a third-world country and hopefully having them recycled by someone there, not to mention having an empty suitcase to fill with trinkets.

Over the course of the two-week journey, though, I noticed a change in her. She seemed tired, frazzled, and rejected. She also tugged on her clothes a lot, as if they didn't quite fit. Finally, I realized that she was wearing not only her old clothes but her old self. The clothes, after being worn many times and now being left behind, were energetically giving her a sense of rejection as well. She was wearing clothes that no longer fit, either physically or emotionally. After we realized this, she was able to buy a couple of new outfits that she loved and leave all the old clothes behind for good. The clothes she found were brighter and fit her well and, even though she only had two outfits for the rest of the journey, she was more energetic and full of joy. Plus, she looked great!

Sometimes, there is an item that has such an attachment to you that you must bring it along. As Jean says:

When traveling I never wear "good" jewelry. I actually purchased a thin gold band that I wear only when traveling in place of my wedding set. Partially this is because I often am traveling to more isolated and poor countries where any display of wealth is arrogant and asking for trouble. But the real reason is that I have long ago requested that my ring protect me. I have set my intent that with this ring on my finger I will be safe.

In the moment-to-moment rush of travel I may forget to ask for protection, so I have found that just slipping my ring on each morning and removing it each night gives me a brief time to affirm my request for safety and joy.

Ritual of Protection

Over the years, I have developed a ritual for protection when I travel, but it also can be used at home. Here is how I do it: Before you leave, find a quiet spot where you feel completely safe and nurtured. Gather a piece of jewelry or a small object you can slip in your pocket (my husband always has a small rock or two in his), again, something that is associated with peace and safety in your mind. For me a wedding band is perfect because I feel safe within the relationship. For others it may be a grandmother's earrings or a button off their old Teddy bear.

Light a candle if you wish, and clear your mind of concerns and the day-to-day worries about packing and getting to the airport or, if you are at home, about the upcoming day. Pick up the object you will be taking with you and cra-

dle it in your hand. *Visualize yourself with the object you have chosen, walking happily down a sidewalk in a town you will soon be traveling in, or perhaps, walking confidently into an important meeting at work. See the ring on your hand or feel the weight of the rock in your pocket. Enjoy the sunshine on your face and the smiles from the people you walk by. Say to yourself: "I am safe and protected on my journey. The people I meet are kind and nurturing. I will make good decisions and care for myself in every way. I affirm that Spirit will watch over me and lead me away from danger and into the light."*

I often find at this point that I can feel my ring singing with energy and warmth. I will come back to the moment, breathe deeply, and enjoy the flame of the candle dancing, slip my ring on my finger ... and have some chocolate. The chocolate is not mandatory, but I do like to ground myself after a ritual with either food or drink ... and why not chocolate?

I really feel that setting your intent and expectations for a safe trip are so important. Whether we consciously remember or not, our unconscious does, and will help us to act in a safe manner. I, of course, also believe that Spirit does offer us protection and signals if we ask for them.

So, how do you know what will enhance your journey? How do we decide to pack a much-loved ring or that we need to lug along a soft pillow? When should we leave behind that iPad or alarm clock or your favorite coffee? That is where your intuition comes in. If you enter a mindful state while packing, you will intuitively know what to put in and what to take out. Your third eye will also tell you what to leave behind because you can't afford to lose it. It may be that your wedding ring is so much a part of you that you hate to take it off. If so, wear it proudly. However, it may also be that your intuition nags you to leave it behind. In that case, trust your intuition to know that it may not be the ring's time to travel.

Of course, international travel is not the only time that we should pack mindfully. I am always amazed at what some people carry in their purses, briefcases, and cars. The same concept applies to these things, which join us on our journeys to work and around our community. A very powerful intuitive exercise is going through one's purse or briefcase and asking, "Does this enhance or detract from my life?" You can also ask, "What effect does carrying this item have on me?"

What did you bring on your life's journey exercise

The goal of this exercise is to see the intuitive messages behind what you are carrying with you in life and then make some decisions about whether what you are carrying serves you.

In order to do this, take a sheet of paper and list everything that you are currently carrying in either your purse, wallet, briefcase, or backpack. If you don't carry any of those things, first of all, congratulations. Second, use what you always carry in your pockets. This item should be something that you carry often when you are out and about. Chose the one thing you never, or at least seldom, leave home without. Don't clean it out first, just list EVERYTHING that is inside including candy wrappers, old receipts, used tissue, and other trash.

For example, when I did this exercise I found the following things in my purse:

1) Two pairs of sunglasses, one prescription and one not

2) A wallet with some money and credit cards

3) Five pens

4) Makeup, lipgloss, and a comb

5) Keys to my house, car, and some no longer remembered places

6) Cell phone

7) Glasses cleaning cloths

   umbrella

After you have made your list, analyze the items by understanding that what you carry when you are on the move is an intuitive symbol for what you think you need on your life's journey. You will need to interpret the meaning of each item based on your feelings about that item and why you always carry it. Here is my interpretation of my purse contents. It will hopefully help you understand how to interpret your own items.

1) I need two pairs of sunglasses because I have two ways of seeing (with and without contact lenses). On my life's journey, I also have two ways of seeing (intuitively and logically). I need both ways and both pairs and they are both equally valuable for me. The message for me is that I also need both ways of seeing ... psychically and logically.

2) My wallet contains enough money and credit cards so that I can take care of myself no matter what happens. I am one of those persons who likes to carry a fair amount of cash ... just in case. My analysis of that is that

I need a lot of security in my life. I can have adventures but also want to make sure I am protected.

3) The pens make sense because I am a writer. I keep many pens just in case I need to make a note of something. Some part of me needs to document my life's journey, not just experience it. I did, though, think five pens was excessive and discarded three of them. I also made sure they all worked, as I don't want my words to dry up just because my pens have.

4) Makeup, combs, and so forth are to disguise myself and make me look better. I know from long experience that, although I am a very public person, I also need plenty of privacy and time to myself. When I put on my stage face I have a sense of being disguised and yet still recognizable. It makes me feel safe.

5) Keys always symbolize our ability to come and go freely. Carrying keys to things you enter or use each day is a symbol of freedom. Holding onto and carrying keys to things you no longer even own is a symbol of holding onto the past. After interpreting that message, I threw away the keys that I couldn't identify and immediately felt freer. Plus, my purse was lighter.

6) A cell phone is an item that represents instantaneous communication. Phones, especially smart phones, are symbolic of wanting to be connected to your spirit guides and other unseen helpers. As with our guides and spirits though, we want to have the power to turn it off when it is not needed, or, at least, turn the volume down.

7) I interpreted the glasses cleaning cloth as my need to see things clearly. I am almost obsessed with having clean glasses and perhaps it is because I so long for clear vision of all types.

Use this exercise to learn more about what is important to you and what things are critical for your life's journey ... wherever it takes you. If you found things that no longer serve you (like my unknown keys and excessive pens), toss them away and see how much freedom you feel. Remember, psychic wanderers travel best when they travel with only what they need ... and that is different for each person.

4) Pack an ability to adapt.

Change is inevitable, in life and in travel. Even with the best of plans, a perfect itinerary and a lot of insurance, things will happen that will throw your agenda into chaos. It is then that you will discover how being adaptable is a survival tactic.

I was recently reading about the Golden Cheeked Warbler, a bird that only nests in Ashe juniper trees. Because of various environmental issues, there are fewer and fewer of these trees standing in Texas which is where the birds go to breed. The worry, of course, is that the bird will go extinct.

I am a bird lover and watcher and I feel very sad about this story. I will also admit that a part of me thinks, "Hey, quit being so darn rigid and find another tree for your nest!"

Adaptability is a trait that is highly linked to survival. One reason human beings survived when dinosaurs and others did not is that we could adapt to climate changes. When the ice age came, we moved south ... or at least some of us did. I am pretty sure there were a few of us who thought, "I can't move. I just got the cave decorated exactly how I want it."

For the most part, though, humans have learned to survive in almost every condition, everywhere on earth (along with rats and cockroaches).

When you travel, particularly abroad, there are a myriad of things to which you need to adapt. Traveling often loudly points out to us just how rigid we are. In my case, for example, I NEED good, strong, coffee to start the day. When I travel, though, I find the definition of good coffee varies dramatically from what I believe it to be. I have grudgingly learned to drink other beverages than what I favor, to eat foods I would never touch at home, to sleep on very hard beds and take icy showers. When we have to be, humans are an adaptable lot.

Our world is, in my opinion, poised on the brink of another great change. I don't know what historians will call this new age but I do know that those who will survive and thrive will be the ones who can adapt to the new conditions.

It is a good time to think about new ways to live life and to think of how you can thrive with the changes. I have had countless people tell me that (for various good reasons) they simply can NOT move from their current house, for example, even though they can no longer afford to live there. Rather like the lovely Warbler, they have become so used to a certain way of life that they will not even consider anything else.

I have great sympathy for this and many other plights so many of us are experiencing right now. Still, there is also a part of me that thinks, "Hey, let's all quit being so rigid and gladly take the evolutionary leap our species is making."

5) God is at the bottom of the mountain, too.

Sometimes when we travel it feels as if we must climb every mountain and ford every stream. I think, over the course of many years, I have climbed a dozen Mayan pyramids, several Chinese bell towers, more than a few steeples and innumerable hills, mountains, and stairways. The view from the top is often spectacular. The view from the bottom is wonderful too, it is just different.

On my first trip to Peru we hired a Quechuan Shaman to lead our group. He led us up more mountain paths than I can remember, always doing a marvelous ceremony or healing at the top. After a few days, though, I was so sore and tired I could barely make it out of bed. For him the climbs must have seemed easy. He was wiry and strong and acclimated to the high altitude. To those of us with thin Minnesotan blood and weak knees, the climbs were very challenging.

One day I simply didn't want to climb. As the shaman started up yet another mountain, I turned to him and said, "You know, God is at the bottom of the mountain, too." He laughed and agreed, then took the rest of the group up while I stayed behind to do my own private ceremony.

Travels present us with daily challenges and we must decide which ones we want to take and which we can skip. (Sounds like life again, doesn't it?) Back when I was very young and arrogant, my husband and I were hiking at a spectacular waterfall in Hawaii. As we returned from our climb, a tour bus pulled up for just long enough to allow the passengers to take a photo out of the bus window. Loren and I were righteously indignant, discussing with each other how we hoped we never got to the point where we would not at least leave the bus at such a beautiful place.

Now, as I age, I realize that perhaps that was all some of the passengers were able to do physically. I also know that I would rather go to a place and see it from a bus window than to sit at home and watch it on TV.

A wise psychic wanderer knows her physical limits and then strives to go just a little beyond them. Traveling teaches us that we can do things we didn't think we could do. Then it teaches us that just because we CAN do something doesn't mean that we have to do it.

That wisdom comes home with us, reminding us to push ourselves a bit but not to ride ourselves unmercifully. Traveling also reminds us that we change and what we could do ten years ago might not be possible now. Then, when that depresses us, we are reminded that God, magic, and miracles as well as faeries, ghosts, and spirits all reside at the bottom of the mountain and even in the bus. When we can no longer go to the magic, the magic will come to us.

6) Travel with a plan,
but give it permission to change.

Not long ago I purchased a new car that came complete with a GPS unit. I thought it was a great feature, because I am notorious for getting lost. I must admit, though, that I don't use it much. I think it is because I find it annoying to have someone tell me what to do in such detail.

It seems to bother her (my GPS is clearly female) greatly when I decide to stray from the route she has set up for me. Then, I get irritated at her insistence that I make a legal U-turn as soon as possible and get back on the road she has mapped out for me. Pretty soon, I find myself arguing out loud with my VERY bossy GPS unit. Often, I end up turning her off.

It struck me that I sometimes do the very same thing with my intuition and my guides. I want the guidance they provide, but I also think I know better than they do. I want to vary my route, make my own decisions, and even make illegal U-turns every once in a while.

I believe that we all came into this life with a plan and a purpose. Before we are born, we meet with our guides and our friends in Spirit and map out a plan for our lives. Then, after we are born and as we age, we consciously forget the plan. In some deep part of us, though, the map still exists and our internal GPS continues to remind us when we have strayed too far from our original plan.

In some ways, we all want a road map of life. Many people come to me wanting to know predictions of what will happen next. They want the certainty of a guaranteed outcome … at least as long as it is what they desire. The truth is, life doesn't work that way. We live in a free-will universe. We can turn off the road we mapped out for ourselves, take detours, make unscheduled stops and even do a complete U turn. We can ignore the map, turn off the GPS of life and head in whatever direction we choose.

It seems these two things are contrary to each other. On one hand, we have access to our internal guidance system (our intuition) and our external guidance system (our guides). On the other hand, we have free will to ignore both of these systems. Like most of you, I suspect, I go back and forth between these two ways of being. Sometimes, I even enjoy being lost. After all, many of life's greatest adventures occur spontaneously and without conscious planning. Then again, most of life's greatest disasters occur because we didn't listen to our guidance.

When I travel, I always like to have a plan. I am not one to set off on a journey without a rather certain itinerary. I do, however, allow myself to change it. I build in enough spontaneity to allow for the little delights that appear on the road. I also keep enough certainty to make sure I always have a place to sleep each night and enough money to get me home. I have learned that my comfort level demands both certainty and spontaneity.

I think that is the way I am in life too. I need some security and certainty, but I also crave excitement and adventure. In the end, perhaps we all come to earth to learn about balance. Maybe part of our purpose in coming to this life is to learn to trust our intuition but also embrace free will.

7) When the trip gives you lemons …

About a year ago I booked what I thought would be an easy and relaxing vacation. I had found a cruise that was a very good deal and thought a week of pampering and warmth before Christmas would be perfect. Life, however, doesn't always give you what you expect.

The day before we left, Minneapolis received twenty inches of snow with high winds. Almost every flight was canceled. We showed up at the airport at six a.m. the next day to find yet more cancellations, de-icings, and full planes. After a very long day, we arrived in Miami an hour after our ship had left without us. Exhausted and hungry, our luggage lost and with no trip insurance, we decided just to forget the cruise and go home. Then we learned that the same cancellations and bad weather meant that all the flights home were booked and we couldn't fly home for three days.

At that point a very kind ticketing agent and guardian angel said just the right words. "You are here now, why not make the best of it?" After getting some food in us, we were able to make lemonade from life's lemons. We booked a flight to St. Thomas, found a hotel there at a decent rate and relaxed. Three days later we were able to pick up the remainder of our cruise from St. Thomas. We kept repeating the mantra "It is only money," and went on to have a lovely time. Oh, and our luggage finally found us.

As a psychic, I was kicking myself for NOT knowing this was going to happen. Still, what would I have done if I had known? The parameters I have set on my intuitive knowing are: "Don't tell me something unless I can do something about it or I need to know it." In this case, there really was nothing I could have done. A snowstorm is an act of God and life, as well as trips, sometimes just gives us lemons.

At home or traveling, all of us have days and times like this. Maybe what we need in those instances is a guardian angel who looks at us and says, "Well, you are here NOW. Why not make the best of it?"

Jean and I have been blessed to travel with many amazing companions over the years. Here she describes our good friend Wayne, who epitomizes the word optimistic.

We have a wonderful friend, Wayne Hartman, whom we met on a trip to India almost twenty years ago. A Southern gentleman, he is also the best traveler I have ever met. He finds charm and joy in almost every experience as he wanders about with his old camera from the 1970s, meeting local people and seeing the world as his oyster.

Where I find fault in a change in itinerary or the weather, he will find the positive. We spent the night in a storage area in the Mumbai airport, trying to sleep on the floor with our suitcases as pillows. Everyone else was being grouchy, Wayne was talking about what an original experience we were having and taking photos of the rats. The rest of us tossed and turned and worried, but our night was accompanied by the gentle snores coming from Wayne's direction. He took it all in stride, and was much better prepared to face the next day's thirty-hour flight.

When Wayne visits us in Minnesota he brings the same traveler's mindset with him and helps me to see our beautiful state in a new way. He revels in the giant loon statue on the roadside, Paul Bunyan, and the SPAM museum in the same way he enjoyed the Taj Mahal. We were in Minot, ND, together and he had me appreciating the city for its heritage and people within moments. For the first time I noticed the unique culture and layout of the city.

He always gets lost, he always ends up in dicey situations, he always makes a new friend and has a new story. I do not know where I first heard the saying, "You know you are a true traveler when you have learned to enjoy the detours," but I always think of Wayne and the constant laughter he brings to our travels.

My friend Steve is another example of someone who has made a lot of lemonade out of some tough circumstances. He traveled quite extensively in his youth and in his business all over the United States and Europe. Then, like a lot of us, he dedicated his life to family and career and put foreign traveling on hold. Unfortunately, diabetes and its consequences, including two strokes and other issues, left Steve with significant physical challenges. After his balance made walking almost impossible without using a walker, Steve was certain that part of life was over for him. When he began to exercise with his treadmill, he was better able to get around but never thought he would travel extensively again.

I encouraged him to try traveling again, starting with a trip to London where he went to Stonehenge, Bath, and Avon. Much to his surprise, he discovered he not only could do things he had not believed were possible, but he flourished doing them. Nowadays, it is rare for him to not have a trip in his planning hopper.

He can't, of course, do all the things that he used to do. Then again, not many of us can. But, he tells me, the joy of sitting at a sidewalk café in Barcelona, sipping a sangria, eating tapas and watching the world go by is equal to climbing the Spanish steps or hiking the hills.

So many people tell me they long to travel but_____ _____ (fill in the blanks). Whether it is physical challenges, financial difficulties, work and family demands, or any other of a dozen reasons, many of us put off traveling until those issues are resolved. The thing about issues, though, is that when one is resolved another one surfaces. Being a psychic wanderer is less about the destination than it is about the experience. As Henry Miller once said, *"One's destination is never a place, but a new way of seeing things."* If you can't afford to travel very far, use your third eye to take you on a journey in your neighborhood. If your knees are too weak to climb the pyramid, sit and ponder its beauty from the base. Take your children on adventures around the neighborhood. The payoff for this is an increased sense of wonder, a heightening of your intuitive ability, and an ever-increasing joy in living.

8) Take time to smell the roses ... and the garbage.

We all have our favored ways of seeing the world. Some of us are highly aware of the emotions of others, while some people seem oblivious to all but the most obvious feelings. Some people remember things better if they hear them, others must see them in print, while some remember colors. I am very aware of scents and apparently have a finely developed sense of smell. I am not sure if this is a blessing or a curse, since it seems there is more garbage than roses in the world. Sometimes, when I am remembering a trip, the thing I remember most is the scent of the country. One of the most effective things you can do when traveling is to add other ways of sensing the world to your most commonly used methods. It is easier to expand your methods when you are out of your day-to-day environment, since your senses are more naturally acute and aware.

Here, Jean describes how her "best" way of seeing the world has been changed and enhanced by traveling.

The term sightseeing has a very special meaning for me. It has changed and evolved as I have traveled. I am a words person, I have always had an affinity for the verbal and written word. I began reading when I was four years old. I naturally feel the power of certain words spoken aloud and have a personal mantra for almost every situation. If the words are set to music ... perfect! I can always remember them.

I have a very hard time with visualizations and meditations because I cannot seem to see with my mind's eye. I often have to literally write the words on a blackboard in my mind, or see a meditation as a marquee scroll of words. When someone says waterfall, I do not see a waterfall so much as I see the word and hear the sound of a waterfall.

After visiting a museum I would be able to tell you what every posted description said, but perhaps not be able to describe the work of art itself. I could quote back the advertisements and streets signs seen from a bus, but miss the tree-lined boulevard.

Travel has challenged me to step out of my comfort zone of words and into situations where everything is visual, auditory, and olfactory. When one does not understand either the written or spoken language surrounding one, all the other senses are sharpened. Facial and hand gestures, tone of voice, slight actions, all suddenly speak volumes.

This was very true in Thailand, the first travel experience where I truly allowed myself to let go of words and practice just the moment. Our small group had taken a boat up the Chiang Rai River to a hill tribe indigenous settlement. These people lived very remotely, without electricity or telephones, and were accessible only by water. They lived in raised huts and ate what they grew or trapped in the surrounding jungle. We toured their village and watched them living their lives. The experience was very surreal, as it felt more than a little like being at a zoo.

I left the group and sat on a log. Soon an elderly woman came to join me. Like the rest of the tribe she wore very little clothing but had on an elaborate headdress. She pointed to my baseball cap and laughed, I pointed to her headdress and clapped. We then exchanged our names, our ages, how many children we had and much more information. All without a single common, understandable word being shared.

I have rarely been to a country where I could not understand enough to get along and stay safe, order meals, or find a companion. A smile, two or three words of the local language....that is all that is needed to make a friend.

By the way, the elderly woman was actually only forty-eight. I was forty-two at the time. Believe me, we are blessed to live the lives we have with dental and health care, nutrition, and our basic needs met.

Looking through the camera lens was another huge stretch outside of my comfort zone. I adore photographs and the thought of capturing a moment in time, a picture that can bring me always back to a moment. Hmmmm, maybe that is because I have such difficulty picturing memories in my mind?

My perfectionism and insecurity made photography so frightening to me. I seemed to never be able to capture the moment the way writing and journaling did. I could hide my journals away, but knew I would share the photos I had taken and risk them being judged.

My first real try at photography was at the Forbidden City in Beijing. Kathryn has written how chaotic and crowded that day was, and here I was fighting claustrophobia yet determined to capture the majesty of the Imperial City on my roll of 35 millimeter film (reluctantly, I admit that this was in 1997 ... before digital cameras). The immensity of the City was too much for me, I had to step back and bring the totality down to the knowable. My favorite photo is of a single bronze *dragon embedded on a peeling doorway, perfectly polished in the midst of the dust and disrepair of the rest of the complex.*

Dragon door in the Forbidden City.

Now I find that it is often the photos of the small and mundane that capture the divine essence of a place for me.

Ways to challenge your senses

Challenge yourself to see more than you usually see. Pretend you are describing a place to a person back home. Phone your imaginary friend and describe the light falling through the trees or the smells of the incense in a temple.

Use a sense that you normally would not use to experience a new place. I visited India with my husband many years ago and a friend sent us a recording of the sounds of Delhi he had taken on the street with us. The overwhelming sounds were amazing, and I could honestly not remember it being that way. Horns honking, people yelling, the temple *bells ringing, cows mooing, motorcycles … how could I have not noticed that perfect symphony that was India?*

I am now totally addicted to taking photography, and am starting to challenge myself to step out from behind the camera, to enjoy and remember moments without the filter of the camera lens. I am trying to take a photo with my mind's eye instead, and capture it in my memory.

Whether you are at home or abroad, take time to expand and use more of your senses than you are accustomed to using. Ask yourself what you are smelling, listen for the distant sounds, look at the tiny things as well as the large. Your trip, no matter how small or large, will become an adventure in sensual discovery.

chapter twelve

*As you move through this life and this
world you change things slightly,
you leave marks behind, however small.
And in return, life—and travel—
leaves marks on you.*

—ANTHONY BOURDAIN

It's a Small World After All

One of the things that traveling and intuition have in common is that they both work better if you are able to suspend your judgment of things. Intuitive information tends to come without any value judgment attached to it. Our intuition gives us messages without any sense of good or bad, right or wrong. Sometimes though, after getting this information, our conscious minds jump in, placing judgment on what we receive. In contrast, the actual vision or words or feelings never carry a sense of rightness or wrongness. That is because intuitive information is valueless. It is never right or wrong...good or bad. It simply is.

Similarly, as psychic wanderers we see and experience many things that are not common to people in their daily lives. Sometimes, the mores and practices of a different country run contrary to our value systems and it is very difficult to accept them. Still, we are in their country and, at least as much as possible, being a psychic wanderer requires us to accept things without judging them. You don't have to travel far for this to be true. The values of a bar, casino, church, political meeting, or your in-laws may not match yours. It is always wise, no matter where you are, to remember when you are the guest and not the host. When you are a guest, whether at your neighbor's picnic or in a foreign land, they are the ones who get to make the rules.

My two weeks on safari in Kenya was one of the most enjoyable experiences of my life. Kenya is a land of spectacular beauty and great contrast. The magnificence of the wildlife and the scenery is breathtaking: the poverty and crime are appalling. In some ways it is a perfect microcosm of this journey we call life.

One day we were privileged to be able to visit a village of the Samburu tribe. The Samburu are a seminomadic people who herd mainly cattle but also keep sheep and goats. Water is a rare commodity and so milk and cattle blood are drunk quite often. The village consists of simple mud huts and the people live in a way that runs counter to many of my values. The marriages are all arranged and the elder men take many wives, primarily young girls. Most disturbing to me is their practice of cutting a girl's clitoris and labia as a rite of passage. I had read about this practice before leaving home and wondered how I would be able to face the people who did such things.

When we arrived in the village we were met by a dozen or so men and women and invited to join them in a dance. We were also invited into their homes so we could see how they lived. The joy and acceptance on their faces did not reflect the sadness I had expected to see.

Kathryn with the Samburu women.

One woman came up to me, took my hand and invited me to join in the dance. For a short time, as we danced, I felt as if I was a part of the tribe. Despite their lifestyle and practices being completely foreign to me, I also was able to step out of my judgment for a moment and see life as they saw it.

While I certainly do not condone the practices of clitoridectomy or underage marriage, I also intuitively knew that there is a time and a place for judgment and that, while I was a guest in their village, it was not the time to make those calls. Part of being a psychic wanderer is seeing with nonjudging eyes and then, upon returning home, taking steps to help if you wish to do so.

I had the same feeling in Peru when visiting the Uros people who live on created reed islands on Lake Titicaca. The

Uros people construct the islands they live upon by weaving dried reeds into large floating mats. The larger islands house about ten families while the smaller ones are less than 100 yards wide and hold only two or three. The islands continually need to be maintained and most last only about thirty years. Nowadays, they are a major tourist attraction.

The most striking thing for me was how COLD it was on the islands. I was wishing for a parka while the villagers were all walking around in bare feet. Lake Titicaca is high in the Andes and has alpine temperatures that seldom reach more than 50 degrees F. All I could think of when I was visiting there was how anyone could live on tiny reed islands, shoeless, in that climate. I HATE being cold and wondered if I, as a tourist, was encouraging them to stay on the islands and to suffer what, to me, was a horrendously cold life.

Sometimes it seems as if it is easier just not to see things that disturb us. Watching things on television or reading about them allows us distance. Holding a person's hand while they dance with you or walking with them on a small island makes it very real.

Not long ago I was conducting a workshop when an audience member asked, "If life in the Spirit realm is so wonderful, why do we bother to come to earth?" The answer given at that time was that earth was a school and that we come here to learn many lessons. This is true, but not the total answer. I think we also come here to experience joy despite the often difficult circumstances of life. It is a challenge I believe we signed up to take and a way to evolve on our spiritual journey.

Recently I read a book in which the author interviewed many famous spiritual leaders. One of the questions he asked each one was: "What do you think is the purpose of life?"

He received many different answers, but my favorite was from the Dalai Lama. He said: "The purpose of life is joy."

Which reminded me of my experiences in Kenya and Lake Titicaca and so many other places in the world where I have seen so much poverty, illness, and suffering. Early on in my travels I realized I could approach other cultures in two ways. I could focus on the beauty or I could focus on the poverty. I could focus on pain or focus on joy. I chose joy. I think in our day-to-day lives we are also often forced to choose between these things. It is part of why we came to this earth. We get, to a large part, what we most focus upon.

In both Kenya and Peru the air was so fresh it was intoxicating. The power and beauty of the wildlife and scenery was breathtaking. The stars leaped from the skies and landed in my soul. The people's smiles lit up their faces. The only way to fully enjoy these things was to enjoy them in the moment, without judgment and without focusing on the pain that also dwells in those places.

Focusing on Joy

Here is a short exercise in focusing on joy, no matter what the circumstances. Take a moment to sit quietly and think of one way in which your life is challenged. Perhaps your job is stressful and boring or maybe your relationship with your mother-in-law is not as good as you would like. Let your mind create a scenario in which you were seeing or experiencing this person, situation, or thing for the first time. Imagine you are a traveler from another land who has just walked into your workplace or met your mother-in-law. Then, focus on the joyful things about each. What would your traveler see with her fresh eyes? What beauty or joyfulness could she focus on?

Does your workplace have a nice break room or do you have a good friend at the desk next to you? Would a traveler from another land be jealous of your new computer or your comfortable chair? Maybe your traveler would see your mother-in-law as generous with gifts or that she is a great cook or has a quirky sense of humor. Focus on the joyful things that a stranger might see when watching you interact with that person or doing that job. Let the visualization work as long as it can and feel your heart and spirit lighten. Then, when you return to that relationship or job in real life, try to approach it with the eyes of a psychic wanderer. Be detached, nonjudgmental, and use your third eye to view the situation. It is funny how peeling paint on an old door in China is charming but on my own front door is disturbing. Sometimes it helps me to simply remind myself no matter where I am, "This really doesn't matter. I am just a wanderer here." Try it. You may be surprised to see how much easier life becomes.

It is possible for two people to take the very same trip, one focusing on the poverty, the crime, the suffering, the poaching, and the loss of ecosystems, while the other focuses on the people's happiness, the amazing scenery, and the ancient history of the places. All of the above problems are very real and valid issues in most countries, including your own. They most definitely need to be addressed.

Just not at the moment when I am wandering. Not at a time when I can gaze into the eyes of a gazelle or lose myself in the constellations of a clear night sky. Those are times to bathe in joy. Changing the world can wait. Maybe bathing in joy does change the world.

Sometimes I think that those of us who deal with spiritual matters forget the pure and simple joy of a beautiful day. Yet my feeling joy has never robbed another of that sensation. In the same way, my feeling sorrow and pity has done nothing to help the person for whom I am sad. So, I bring my joy home with me from Peru, Kenya, and around the world. It is my best souvenir ever!

There is plenty of time when we get home to put our time, money, and power into things and organizations that can help aid the world's suffering. Seeing things that disturb us is a good motivator for action when we return home. It is impossible to travel without being changed in some fashion. You can no longer turn a blind eye to something once you have held its hand.

There is a good argument to be made for not supporting countries that allow atrocities to exist. After all, when we travel to a country we are contributing to its economy, and usually not to the people who actually need the money. I also think, though, that our very presence in a country changes it in some way, hopefully for the better.

Years ago I traveled for a few weeks in Morocco. Because I am an independent and headstrong woman, traveling in a Muslim country is a challenge at times. Loren and I were walking the streets of Casablanca one beautiful day when we decided to stop into a local café for a cup of coffee. As soon as we entered it was apparent that women were not welcome there. All the men (and there were only men in the café) turned their chairs toward me and stared the entire time I was there. It was tremendously uncomfortable for me and yet my pride would not allow me to leave until I finished my drink. Still, I was pleased that they had served me and some small part of me felt I was making a statement, although I am still not sure what.

Do I think I made a difference in the culture? No, not at all. I like to think, though, that it could not have hurt. Those of us who live in the United States and other western nations have been blessed to have been born here. Or, in my way of thinking, we were smart to choose this country as our birthplace. I also have to remember that other cultures usually feel that way about their country of origin.

Sometimes just our contact with the local people, our conversations, and yes, even our purchases, can make a positive difference. Years ago Jean and Fred learned this in a tiny town in Mexico.

Ten years ago my husband and I, along with our best friends, rented a house in a small fishing village near Cancun. Across the street was a tiny roadside stand where a local artisan sold her wares.

Fred was immediately drawn to the shop's display of stones and rocks that Ixchel, a Mayan Indian, used in her jewelry. She was so excited by his interest as most people who bought from her saw it only as ornamentation. I said, in my limited Spanish, that Fred was enchanted by rocks. Ixchel said, in her limited English, "I also am enchanted by the stones. I work with silver because of money, but my magic is in the rocks." She pressed a polished stone into Fred's hand, saying, "Magic can only be given freely, never paid for," as she rejected payment. Fred reached into his pocket and gifted her with a piece of opal that he had found in Iceland.

The next day a small girl appeared at our doorway and requested we come with her to the shop. Thankfully our friend, Colleen, spoke Spanish. I am not sure I would have followed the girl otherwise. It was Ixchel's thirty-sixth birthday, and she wanted to share the cake with us. It was very, very sweet....both literally and spiritually.

Later in the week we returned to the stall to buy something from her. Ixchel told us that her mother was a shaman, and that her son also had the gift, but he was being seduced away from it by the music and videos.

She told us how she searched for rocks when the moon and sun were right because that was when she could feel the rock's energy the best. She encouraged Fred to keep searching for rocks and stones that brought him magic and energy, but to remember that rocks never truly belong to a person. "They may disappear to go to the next person who needs them, so never mourn a lost rock," she told him.

Ixchel and I discussed how she felt about American tourism and how it was changing her small village. "Each stranger brings a gift to Mexico that we must try to understand. Puerto Morelos has plenty of magic to share with the visitors." Her prayer was that the development would not destroy the huge mangrove coastal regions, saying, "At night I hear them crying—they know they will not be here long. They do not cry for themselves, but for the people who destroy them."

We both cried, "En todo mundo."

"The world cries with us," she said.

I bought a necklace and earring set from her, along with a silver cross for my brother. The total was less than twenty-five dollars, yet each time I wear them I am transported back to a connection and remember lessons well learned. Magic cannot be destroyed, only given freely and it goes where it will. Travelers bring gifts beyond their money spent, and take home gifts that are much more important than the tchotchkes and souvenirs they buy.

Jean making friends.

We will never fully know how our presence in a place changes that place. For every purchase we make, every person we talk to, every place we go; we leave our energy. It does indeed change the world a little. Being conscious about how we affect places also does an amazing thing for us. It makes us think. It makes us listen to our intuition. It makes us better people. It turns us into psychic wanderers.

Recently I heard someone say, "The last place you want to be is in a first-class seat heading where you don't want to go." That is, in my opinion, a thought worth pondering at this time in Earth's history. When I asked my guides, the Light Collective, what they thought about that statement, they said, "Your country is in that seat, Kathryn."

All of us in the United States, no matter how poor we may think we are, are traveling through time in first-class seats. I often think of that when visiting countries such as Kenya, Cambodia, and so many others. These are lands of incredible beauty and power and, of course, great poverty. We have laughingly joked that the locals often view tourists as "wallets on legs." Our wealth is beyond their comprehension.

I am not one to glamorize poverty. If I lived in poverty I would not see it as noble. I would be the first one to want a television and indoor plumbing. Certainly everyone deserves a safe source of drinking water and an adequate amount of food.

I also know that, except for spending a lot of money while traveling, there isn't a great deal I personally can do about third-world poverty. What I do have control over is my own life and I want to make sure I am spiritually heading in the direction that I want to go. I don't want to return to Spirit just to discover that I spent this lifetime in a very nice environment without accomplishing much of anything.

We are entering one of our planet's most significant cycles in thousands of years. I believe many of us chose to incarnate on this planet during this time for that reason. Maybe we are just adrenaline junkies, but maybe we have some part to play in the upcoming events.

You will hear a lot of prophecy in the next few years and much of what you hear may be frightening. I don't believe the Earth is going to end soon, nor do I believe it will become a Heaven on Earth. There already is a Heaven and it isn't here. We came to Earth to learn and grow, and we will return to Spirit when we are ready to take a little break.

If, as so many say, earth is a school, then what will our graduation look like? I believe it will be a transition from one way of thinking to another. Like a graduation from high school, we will venture forth, each on our own path. Some of us may go on to further learning. Some of us may find a new job. Others may take an extended vacation. All of these paths are perfect….as long as we head down our paths with intention and direction. All of us are psychic wanderers and all our wanderings take us on different yet equal challenging and yet joyful journeys.

The upcoming years will challenge us to decide where we want to go. We are among the elite. We are traveling on a first-class ticket. Very few of us really need to worry about obtaining food, water, and shelter. With that comes the responsibility of being conscious, awake, and alive. So, grab your passports, comfortable shoes, and sunscreen, and prepare for the adventure of many a lifetime.

Several years ago, I spent two weeks in China traveling with Feng Shui expert Carole Hyder and a group of her students. Each morning Carole would start the day by having the group chant the Buddhist Calming Mantra from the Heart Sutra (*Gatay, Gatay, Para Gatay, Para Sum Gatay, Bodhi Swaha*).

As far as I can tell, the meaning of the words is this:

Traveling, Traveling

Still Traveling

Traveling yet some more

and then arriving.

It has been a number of years now since that trip to China, yet those words still echo in my brain. When I think of it, I guess I have been doing the Gatays all my life. Traveling, traveling, still traveling…

I am not sure what happens when we arrive. I have a fantasy of arriving in Heaven (whatever that is) with a suitcase in one hand and a passport tightly grasped in the other. "Have I arrived?" I will ask. I hear this gentle answer: "Not yet, Kathryn."

No, I am not yet ready to arrive. And so Jean and I end this book with a wish for you all.

Gatay, Gatay, para Gatay.

Still traveling.

To Write to the Authors

If you wish to contact the author or would like more information about this book, please write to the author in care of Llewellyn Worldwide Ltd. and we will forward your request. Both the author and publisher appreciate hearing from you and learning of your enjoyment of this book and how it has helped you. Llewellyn Worldwide Ltd. cannot guarantee that every letter written to the author can be answered, but all will be forwarded. Please write to:

Kathryn Harwig & Jean Harwig
⁒ Llewellyn Worldwide
2143 Wooddale Drive.
Woodbury, MN 55125-2989

Please enclose a self-addressed stamped envelope for reply, or $1.00 to cover costs. If outside the U.S.A., enclose an international postal reply coupon.

Ignite Your Psychic Intuition

An
A to Z Guide
to Developing Your
Sixth Sense

Teresa Brady

Ignite Your Psychic Intuition
An A to Z Guide to Developing Your Sixth Sense
Teresa Brady

Developing your psychic powers doesn't have to take a lot of time and patience. *Ignite Your Psychic Intuition* proves that we can easily tap into our sixth sense, even with the busiest of lifestyles.

In this innovative and easy-to-use guide, Teresa Brady demystifies psychic and intuitive development and step-by-step shows you how to unlock and heighten your extrasensory perception. Designed in an A-to-Z format, this book offers twenty-six practical teaching tools, one for each letter of the alphabet. Discover the four main types of intuitive communication—clairvoyance, clairaudience, clairsentience, and clair-cognizance—and how to use them to enhance your life.

Beginners and experienced practitioners looking for new ideas will enjoy developing their higher senses through white light bathing, energy scans, salt showers, directed dreaming, chakra cleansing, and crystal gazing.

978-0-7387-2170-5, 288 pp., 5 x 7 **$14.95**

Discover *your* Psychic Type

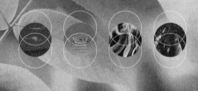

Developing and Using Your Natural Intuition

SHERRIE DILLARD

Discover Your Psychic Type
Developing and Using Your Natural Intuition
Sherrie Dillard

Intuition and spiritual growth are indelibly linked, according to professional psychic and therapist Sherrie Dillard. Offering a personalized approach to psychic development, this breakthrough guide introduces four different psychic types and explains how to develop the unique spiritual capabilities of each.

Are you a physical, mental, emotional, or spiritual intuitive? Take Dillard's insightful quiz to find out. Discover more about each type's intuitive nature, personality, potential physical weaknesses, and more. There are guided meditations for each kind of intuitive, as well as exercises to hone your psychic skills. Remarkable stories from the author's professional life illustrate the incredible power of intuition and its connection to the spirit world, inner wisdom, and your higher self.

From psychic protection to spirit guides to mystical states, Dillard offers guidance as you evolve toward the final destination of every psychic type: union with the divine.

978-0-7387-1278-9, 288 pp., 5³⁄₁₆ x 8   **$14.95**

KATHRYN HARWIG

The

RETURN

of

INTUITION

Awakening Psychic Gifts
in the Second Half of Life

The Return of Intuition
Awakening Psychic Gifts in the Second Half of Life
Kathryn Harwig

Natural psychic sensitivity is often associated with children. However, *The Return of Intuition* reveals a little-known, widespread phenomenon of profound intuitive awakening occurring in adults—usually around the age of fifty.

Bringing this remarkable trend to light is psychic medium Kathryn Harwig, who has helped clients nationwide understand, nurture, and embrace their newfound psychic awareness. Their inspiring stories highlight what triggers this life-changing gift—usually illness or the death of a loved one—and how it can be used to aid others, receive messages from friends and family in spirit, and begin life anew with confidence, courage, and clarity. Affirming the joys of aging, this unique spiritual guide offers comfort and support to the elders of our society, encouraging them to reclaim their once-revered roles—as the crone, shaman, and sage—by passing on spiritual wisdom to a new generation.

978-0-7387-1880-4, 216 pp., 5³⁄₁₆ x 8   **$15.95**

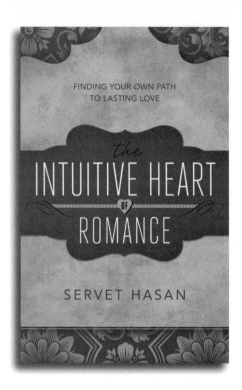

FINDING YOUR OWN PATH
TO LASTING LOVE

the
INTUITIVE HEART
OF
ROMANCE

SERVET HASAN

The Intuitive Heart of Romance
Finding Your Own Path to Lasting Love
Servet Hasan

Relationships are drastically changing. Women have more choices than ever when it comes to careers, marriage, kids, and love. Given these new possibilities, how can women create healthy, lasting relationships? The answer is profoundly spiritual.

Servet Hasan offers fresh, practical advice in this spiritual guide to the evolving world of love and relationships. Soul-centered meditations and exercises help women to access and develop their innate intuitive gifts to strengthen and deepen romantic relationships.

As they learn to use their intuition, women will gain insight into commitment, sacred sex, relinquishing fears, resolving conflicts, moving beyond dead-end relationships, releasing repressed beliefs, and creating a deeply spiritual bond with their partners.

978-0-7387-2584-0, 288 pp., 5³⁄₁₆ x 8　　　　　**$15.95**

So
You
Want
to Be
a
PSYCHIC
INTUITIVE?

A Down-to-Earth Guide

Alexandra Chauran

So You Want to Be a Psychic Intuitive?
A Down-to-Earth Guide
Alexandra Chauran

Dependable guidance, communication with departed loved ones, helping friends and family—the lifelong rewards of a strong psychic connection are countless. Whether you're a beginner or already in touch with your intuition, this encouraging, conversational, and hands-on guide can help you strengthen your psychic skills. Featuring illustrative anecdotes and easy exercises, you'll learn how to achieve a receptive state, identify your source of information, receive messages, and interpret coincidences, dreams, and symbols. Step-by-step instructions make it easy to try a variety of psychic techniques and divination, such as telepathy, channeling, spirit communication, automatic writing, and scrying. There's also practical advice for wisely applying your enhanced psychic skills personally and professionally.

978-0-7387-3065-3, 264 pp., 5³⁄₁₆ x 8   **$14.95**